How to ADHD

Empowering parents to Nurture ,Guide and celebrate their ADHD Children's Unique Abilities

Table of Content

Chapter 1:

*Understanding ADHD: An
Introduction to the Neurodevelopmental
Disorder*

Understanding ADHD: An Introduction to the Neurodevelopmental Disorder

ADHD, or Attention-Deficit/Hyperactivity Disorder, is a complex neurodevelopmental disorder that impacts individuals across various aspects of their lives. It typically manifests during childhood and can persist into adulthood. The disorder is characterized by difficulties in maintaining attention, controlling impulsive behaviors, and often excessive levels of hyperactivity.

Researchers believe that ADHD is caused by a combination of genetic, neurological, and environmental factors. Genetic predisposition plays a significant role, as the disorder tends to run in families. Neurologically, there are differences in the brain structure and function of individuals with ADHD, particularly in areas related to attention regulation, impulse control, and executive functioning.

The symptoms of ADHD are divided into two main categories: inattention and hyperactivity-impulsivity. Inattentive symptoms include struggles with sustaining attention in tasks, easily becoming distracted, making careless mistakes, and struggling to organize tasks or activities. Hyperactivity-impulsivity symptoms involve restlessness, fidgeting, difficulty remaining seated, interrupting others, and impulsive decision-making.

Diagnosing ADHD involves a comprehensive assessment by a qualified healthcare professional, often including input from parents, teachers, and caregivers. There is no single test for ADHD; instead, a combination of interviews, questionnaires, behavioral observations, and medical history analysis is used to make an accurate diagnosis.

Treatment approaches for ADHD are multifaceted and can be tailored to the individual's needs. Behavioral interventions, such as cognitive-behavioral therapy and psychoeducation, help individuals develop strategies to manage their symptoms. For many individuals, medication, like stimulants (e.g., methylphenidate) or non-stimulants (e.g., atomoxetine), can be effective in improving attention and impulse control.

It's important to note that while ADHD poses challenges, it can also bring strengths. Many individuals with ADHD are creative, innovative, and possess a high level of energy. With the right support and strategies, individuals with ADHD can thrive in various areas of their lives, including education, work, and relationships.

In conclusion, ADHD is a neurodevelopmental disorder that affects attention, impulse control, and hyperactivity. It's a complex interplay of genetics, brain structure, and environmental factors. While it presents challenges, proper diagnosis and management can help individuals lead fulfilling lives that capitalize on their unique strengths. If you suspect you or someone you know might have ADHD, seeking professional guidance is crucial for understanding and managing the disorder effectively.

1.1 What is ADHD?

ADHD, or Attention-Deficit/Hyperactivity Disorder, is a neurodevelopmental disorder that primarily affects a person's ability to focus, control impulses, and regulate their level of activity. It typically emerges in childhood and can persist into adulthood. The disorder is characterized by three main types of symptoms:

Inattention: Individuals with ADHD may have difficulty sustaining attention on tasks, organizing activities, and following through on instructions. They might be easily distracted by external stimuli or have difficulty staying focused on tasks that require sustained mental effort.

Hyperactivity: This refers to excessive and often inappropriate levels of physical activity or restlessness. People with ADHD may feel the urge to move constantly, have difficulty remaining seated, or talk excessively.

Impulsivity: Individuals with ADHD may act without thinking, interrupt others, and have difficulty waiting their turn. They might struggle to inhibit inappropriate behaviors, leading to impulsive decisions and reactions.

It's important to note that ADHD is a spectrum disorder, meaning the severity of these symptoms can vary widely from person to person. The causes of ADHD are complex and likely involve a combination of genetic, neurological, and environmental factors. Diagnosis is typically made based on the presence of these symptoms and their impact on daily functioning.

Treatment approaches include behavioral interventions, psychoeducation, and sometimes medication. Behavioral therapy helps individuals develop strategies to manage their symptoms and improve their executive functioning skills. Medications, such as stimulants or non-stimulants, can also be prescribed to help regulate attention and reduce impulsivity.

Overall, ADHD is a multifaceted disorder that can have a significant impact on various aspects of an individual's life, including academic, social, and occupational functioning.

1.2 Prevalence and Diagnosis of ADHD

An in-depth overview of the prevalence and diagnosis of ADHD.

Prevalence of ADHD:
Attention-Deficit/Hyperactivity Disorder (ADHD) is a neurodevelopmental disorder characterized by persistent patterns of inattention, hyperactivity, and impulsivity. The prevalence of ADHD varies across different populations and age groups. Research indicates that ADHD is one of the most common childhood-onset psychiatric disorders, with estimates of prevalence ranging from 5% to 10% globally. It is important to note that ADHD can persist into adulthood, with about 50% to 60% of children with ADHD continuing to exhibit symptoms as adults.

Diagnosis of ADHD:
Diagnosing ADHD is a complex process that involves comprehensive assessment and evaluation. There is no single test that can definitively diagnose ADHD; instead, a combination of clinical interviews,

observations, and standardized rating scales is used to determine if an individual meets the diagnostic criteria.

The diagnostic criteria for ADHD are outlined in the Diagnostic and Statistical Manual of Mental Disorders, Fifth Edition (DSM-5), which categorizes ADHD into three subtypes:

Predominantly Inattentive Presentation
Predominantly Hyperactive-Impulsive Presentation
Combined Presentation (both inattentive and hyperactive-impulsive symptoms)
To meet the criteria for ADHD, an individual must exhibit symptoms that are inconsistent with their developmental level and interfere with their functioning or quality of life. The symptoms must be present for at least six months and occur in two or more settings (e.g., home, school, work).

The diagnosis process typically involves:

Clinical Interviews: Gathering information from the individual, their parents (in the case of children), and significant others to understand the nature and duration of symptoms.

Behavioral Observations: Collecting data on the individual's behavior in different settings to corroborate reported symptoms.

Standardized Rating Scales: Using validated rating scales filled out by parents, teachers, and sometimes the individual themselves, to assess the severity and pervasiveness of ADHD symptoms.

Medical Evaluation: Ruling out other medical or psychological conditions that could be contributing to the symptoms.

Diagnostic Criteria: Comparing the collected information to the DSM-5 criteria to determine if the individual meets the requirements for an ADHD diagnosis.

It's important to note that a comprehensive evaluation is crucial to avoid misdiagnosis, as ADHD symptoms can overlap with other conditions such as anxiety, depression, learning disabilities, and more.

In recent years, discussions have arisen around potential overdiagnosis and underdiagnosis of ADHD, highlighting the need for careful and accurate assessment. The diagnosis of ADHD has significant implications for treatment, education, and support, making it essential to ensure a thorough and accurate evaluation process.

1.3 Common Symptoms and Challenges Faced by Children with ADHD

Children with ADHD often experience a range of common symptoms and challenges that can significantly impact their daily lives and overall well-being. These symptoms are categorized into two main types: inattention and hyperactivity-impulsivity.

Inattention Symptoms:

Difficulty Sustaining Attention: Children with ADHD may struggle to focus on tasks, get easily distracted by unrelated stimuli, or have trouble maintaining attention during activities that require mental effort.
Poor Organization: They might find it challenging to organize tasks, activities, and belongings, leading to messy rooms, missed assignments, and forgetfulness.
Forgetfulness: Children with ADHD often forget important daily responsibilities, such as chores, homework, or appointments, even if they seem enthusiastic initially.
Avoidance of Tasks Requiring Sustained Mental Effort: They may avoid tasks that require prolonged

concentration or effort, such as reading, studying, or completing assignments.

Difficulty Following Instructions: Following multi-step instructions, especially in academic or organized settings, can be a struggle.

Hyperactivity-Impulsivity Symptoms:

Excessive Fidgeting or Restlessness: Children may engage in continuous movement, like tapping their feet or hands, squirming in their seats, or getting up when expected to remain seated.

Difficulty Remaining Quiet: They might frequently talk excessively, interrupt conversations, or have trouble waiting their turn, leading to disruptions in classroom or social settings.

Impulsivity: Children with ADHD often act without thinking of the consequences, blurting out answers, making impulsive decisions, or engaging in risky behavior.

Inability to Stay Engaged in Quiet Activities: Sitting still during activities that require calmness, like reading or playing quiet games, can be challenging.

Challenges Faced:

Academic Struggles: Children with ADHD may experience difficulties in school, such as poor grades, incomplete assignments, and trouble following instructions, which can affect their self-esteem and motivation to learn.

Social Issues: Their impulsive behavior, difficulty regulating emotions, and social awkwardness can lead to strained friendships, isolation, and a sense of not fitting in.

Emotional Dysregulation: Intense emotions, mood swings, and low frustration tolerance are common, causing emotional outbursts that may disrupt relationships and daily functioning.

Executive Function Deficits: Challenges in executive functions, such as planning, time management, and organization, can impact their ability to complete tasks and meet responsibilities.

Low Self-Esteem: Repeated failures and negative feedback can contribute to a sense of inadequacy, lowering their self-esteem and self-confidence.

Family Stress: The demands of parenting a child with ADHD can lead to family stress, as parents often navigate behavioral issues, school struggles, and seek appropriate interventions.

It's important to note that each child with ADHD is unique, and the severity of symptoms and challenges can vary. Early identification, personalized treatment plans, and support from parents, educators, and healthcare professionals can greatly assist children with ADHD in overcoming these obstacles and thriving.

1.4 The Impact of ADHD on Parents and Families

Attention Deficit Hyperactivity Disorder (ADHD) is a neurodevelopmental disorder characterized by persistent patterns of inattention, impulsivity, and hyperactivity that can significantly impact various aspects of an individual's life. While much attention has been given to understanding how ADHD affects the individuals diagnosed with the condition, it's important to recognize that the impact extends beyond the individual to their parents and families. The challenges posed by ADHD can have profound effects on familial dynamics, emotional well-being, and overall quality of life.

Disrupted Family Dynamics: Managing a child with ADHD can introduce a higher level of stress into the family environment. The daily struggles associated with ADHD, such as difficulties in maintaining routines, completing tasks, and following instructions, can disrupt family routines and dynamics. Parents may find themselves constantly addressing behavioral issues and managing impulsive actions, which can lead to strained relationships, conflicts, and misunderstandings among family members.

Emotional Toll: Parents of children with ADHD often experience heightened levels of stress, frustration, and exhaustion. The continuous demands of caregiving, coupled with the unpredictability of ADHD-related behaviors, can take a toll on parents' emotional well-being. Feelings of guilt, inadequacy, and isolation are not uncommon, as parents may blame themselves for their child's struggles or feel socially isolated due to difficulties in socializing or participating in activities.

Financial Strain: The financial impact of ADHD can also be a significant stressor for families. Costs associated with medical evaluations, therapy sessions, medications, and educational support can accumulate over time. Parents may need to allocate additional resources for tutoring, specialized interventions, and other services to support their child's needs, potentially affecting the family's financial stability.

Parental Well-being: The demands of raising a child with ADHD can compromise parents' physical and mental health. Sleep deprivation is common among parents as they navigate sleep disturbances experienced by their child. This chronic lack of sleep can contribute to a decline in parents' overall health. Additionally, the chronic stress associated with managing ADHD-related challenges can increase the risk of anxiety and depression in parents.

Siblings and Family Roles: Siblings of children with ADHD may experience mixed emotions. They might alternate between understanding their sibling's condition and feeling neglected due to the attention their sibling requires. Over time, this dynamic can shape their relationship with their parents and influence their own emotional well-being. Parents may also struggle to divide their attention and resources equitably among all their children, impacting the family's overall equilibrium.

Coping Strategies: Families often develop coping strategies to navigate the challenges of living with ADHD. These strategies may involve implementing structured routines, seeking professional support through therapy and counseling, educating themselves about ADHD, and fostering open communication within the family. Parental support groups can offer a valuable platform for sharing experiences, strategies, and emotional support.

In conclusion, the impact of ADHD on parents and families is multifaceted and extends beyond the individual diagnosed with the disorder. Recognizing the challenges that parents and families face is essential for providing comprehensive support to those affected by ADHD. By acknowledging the emotional, financial, and relational strains, society can better address the unique needs of families living with ADHD and work towards improving their overall well-being.

Chapter 2

The Science Behind ADHD: Exploring the Neurological Factors

ADHD, or Attention-Deficit/Hyperactivity Disorder, is a complex neurodevelopmental disorder that affects both children and adults. Its underlying mechanisms involve a combination of genetic, neurological, and environmental factors. While a comprehensive exploration would require an extensive discussion, I can outline some key points related to the neurological factors involved in ADHD:

Neurotransmitter Imbalance: One of the prominent theories suggests that ADHD is linked to an imbalance in neurotransmitters, which are chemicals that transmit signals between nerve cells in the brain. The neurotransmitters dopamine and norepinephrine play a crucial role in regulating attention, focus, and impulse control. Research indicates that individuals with ADHD might have lower levels of these neurotransmitters or difficulties in their transmission.

Brain Structure and Function: Neuroimaging studies have revealed differences in the brain structure and function of individuals with ADHD. The prefrontal cortex, responsible for executive functions such as planning, decision-making, and impulse control, often shows reduced activation in people with ADHD. Additionally, the basal ganglia, a group of structures involved in regulating motor functions and attention, might also be implicated.

Cortical Networks: ADHD involves altered connectivity within certain brain networks. The default mode network (DMN), which is active when the mind is at rest, and the task-positive network (TPN), active during focused tasks, show atypical interactions in individuals with ADHD. This might contribute to difficulties in shifting between internal thoughts and external tasks.

Genetic Factors: Genetic predisposition is a significant contributor to ADHD. Several genes related to dopamine regulation, synaptic plasticity, and neural development have been associated with the disorder. However, ADHD is likely influenced by multiple genes, and the interplay of these genetic variations contributes to its complexity.

Neurodevelopmental Delays: ADHD is often considered a disorder of neurodevelopment. The brain undergoes significant changes during childhood and adolescence, and disruptions in these processes can lead to ADHD symptoms. The precise nature of these developmental delays and their impact on neural circuits involved in attention and impulse control is an area of ongoing research.

Environmental Factors: Prenatal and early childhood environmental factors, such as maternal smoking during pregnancy, premature birth, exposure to toxins, and early adversity, can also play a role in the development of ADHD. These factors can influence brain development and increase the risk of ADHD symptoms.

Neurotransmitter Receptors: Alongside neurotransmitter levels, the functioning of neurotransmitter receptors is crucial. Individuals with ADHD might have variations in the genes that encode these receptors, affecting their sensitivity to dopamine and norepinephrine.

It's important to note that the exact mechanisms behind ADHD are still being investigated, and the disorder's heterogeneity makes it challenging to pinpoint a single cause. The interplay between genetic predisposition, brain structure and function, neurotransmitter systems, and environmental influences likely contributes to the development and manifestation of ADHD. This understanding is a stepping stone for developing targeted interventions and treatments that address the neurological underpinnings of the disorder.

2.1 The Role of Genetics in ADHD

ADHD, or Attention-Deficit/Hyperactivity Disorder, is a neurodevelopmental disorder characterized by persistent patterns of inattention, hyperactivity, and impulsivity that can significantly impact daily functioning. While the exact causes of ADHD are not fully understood, there is substantial evidence to suggest that genetics play a significant role in its development.

Research studies have consistently shown that ADHD tends to run in families, with a higher prevalence of the disorder among close relatives of individuals with ADHD. Twin studies have been particularly insightful in understanding the genetic contribution to ADHD. Identical twins, who share 100% of their genetic material, are more likely to both have ADHD if one twin is diagnosed with the disorder, compared to fraternal twins who share about 50% of their genetic material.

Several genes have been implicated in ADHD, although no single gene has been identified as the sole cause. These genes are often involved in the regulation of neurotransmitters, which are chemicals that transmit signals in the brain. Dopamine, in particular, has been a focus of ADHD research due to its role in reward and motivation pathways. Variants of genes related to dopamine receptors and transporters have been associated with ADHD risk.

It's important to note that genetics is not the only factor at play. Environmental factors also contribute to the development of ADHD. These can include prenatal exposure to toxins, maternal smoking during pregnancy, low birth weight, premature birth, and early childhood exposure to lead. Additionally, brain injuries, infections, and certain medical conditions can mimic the symptoms of ADHD.

The interplay between genetics and the environment is complex and not fully understood. It's likely that multiple genes, each with a small effect, interact with various environmental factors to increase the risk of ADHD. This complexity makes studying the genetic basis of ADHD challenging, as well as developing targeted treatments based solely on genetics.

In recent years, advancements in genetic research techniques have allowed for the identification of specific genetic variations associated with ADHD susceptibility. This has paved the way for potential personalized treatments that could be tailored to an individual's genetic profile. However, more research is needed to fully understand the mechanisms by which these genetic variations contribute to ADHD and how they interact with environmental factors.

In conclusion, while genetics plays a significant role in the development of ADHD, it is a complex disorder influenced by both genetic and environmental factors. Understanding the genetic basis of ADHD can offer insights into its underlying mechanisms, improve diagnostic accuracy, and potentially lead to more effective treatment strategies in the future.

2.2 Neurotransmitters and their Influence on ADHD

Neurotransmitters play a significant role in influencing various aspects of brain function, including attention and behavior, which are central to understanding ADHD (Attention-Deficit/Hyperactivity Disorder). ADHD is a complex neurodevelopmental disorder characterized by persistent patterns of inattention, impulsivity, and hyperactivity that interfere with daily functioning. While the exact cause of ADHD is not fully understood, neurotransmitter imbalances have been implicated in its development and manifestation.

Key neurotransmitters associated with ADHD include dopamine, norepinephrine, and serotonin. These neurotransmitters are essential for transmitting signals between nerve cells in the brain and regulating mood, attention, and motivation.

Dopamine: Dopamine is closely linked to the brain's reward and pleasure pathways. It is involved in regulating motivation, focus, and the ability to experience pleasure from activities. In individuals with ADHD, there is evidence of reduced dopamine activity in certain brain regions. This could contribute to difficulties in sustaining attention, as well as impulsive and hyperactive behaviors.

Norepinephrine: Norepinephrine, also known as noradrenaline, is involved in the body's "fight or flight" response. It helps regulate alertness, arousal, and attention. Some research suggests that abnormalities in norepinephrine systems may lead to issues with sustained attention and impulsivity in individuals with ADHD.

Serotonin: Serotonin is often associated with mood regulation, but it also plays a role in controlling impulsivity, aggression, and emotional responses. Some studies have suggested that alterations in serotonin pathways may contribute to emotional dysregulation and impulsive behavior observed in ADHD.

Genetic factors are believed to influence the functioning of these neurotransmitter systems. Research indicates that individuals with ADHD may have genetic variations that affect the production, release, or reuptake of these neurotransmitters, contributing to the symptoms of the disorder.

Stimulant medications, such as methylphenidate and amphetamines, are commonly prescribed to treat

ADHD. They work by increasing the availability of dopamine and norepinephrine in the brain, which helps improve attention and impulse control. Non-stimulant medications, like atomoxetine, target norepinephrine levels and can also be effective in managing ADHD symptoms.

It's important to note that while neurotransmitter imbalances play a role in ADHD, other factors such as brain structure, genetics, environmental influences, and cognitive processes also contribute to the disorder. ADHD is a complex condition, and its treatment often involves a multimodal approach that may include behavioral interventions, counseling, and medication.

In conclusion, neurotransmitters like dopamine, norepinephrine, and serotonin have a significant influence on the development and manifestation of ADHD symptoms. However, the interplay between genetics, brain structure, and environmental factors also contributes to the complexity of this disorder. Ongoing research aims to deepen our understanding of these mechanisms and improve the effectiveness of treatments for individuals with ADHD.

2.3 Brain Structure and Function in Individuals with ADHD

An in-depth overview of brain structure and function in individuals with Attention Deficit Hyperactivity Disorder (ADHD).

ADHD is a neurodevelopmental disorder that primarily affects executive functions, which are cognitive processes responsible for goal-directed behaviors, inhibition of impulsive actions, working memory, and attention control. While the exact cause of ADHD is not fully understood, research has shown that there are differences in brain structure and function between individuals with ADHD and those without the disorder.

Brain Structure Differences:
Neuroimaging studies, such as MRI and fMRI scans, have revealed structural differences in the brains of individuals with ADHD. Some key findings include:

Smaller Prefrontal Cortex: The prefrontal cortex, responsible for executive functions, is often found to be smaller in individuals with ADHD.

Basal Ganglia Abnormalities: The basal ganglia, which plays a role in motor control and reward processing, also shows differences in size and connectivity.

Cerebellar Involvement: The cerebellum, traditionally associated with motor coordination, has been found to have connections to cognitive processes affected by ADHD.

Neurotransmitter Function:

ADHD has been linked to imbalances in neurotransmitters, particularly dopamine and norepinephrine. These neurotransmitters are involved in regulating attention, motivation, and arousal. The lower availability or dysregulation of these neurotransmitters could contribute to the difficulties in sustaining attention and controlling impulses seen in ADHD.

Neural Networks and Connectivity:

Functional connectivity studies have shown that individuals with ADHD often exhibit altered connectivity patterns within the default mode network (associated with mind-wandering and internal reflection) and the task-positive network (associated with goal-directed tasks). These altered connections could explain the challenges individuals with ADHD face in maintaining attention on tasks.

Cortical Activation and Inhibition:

Research using EEG and fMRI has demonstrated that individuals with ADHD might have differences in cortical activation and inhibition processes. This could relate to difficulties in filtering out irrelevant information and maintaining sustained attention.

Genetic Factors:
Genetic studies have also indicated a hereditary component in ADHD. Certain genes involved in neural development, neurotransmitter regulation, and synaptic plasticity have been associated with an increased risk of developing ADHD.

It's important to note that while these brain differences are commonly observed in individuals with ADHD, there can be significant variation between individuals. Additionally, these neurological differences are not deterministic but rather contribute to the overall complex picture of ADHD. Treatments for ADHD often include behavioral interventions, psychoeducation, counseling, and, in some cases, medication to help regulate neurotransmitter imbalances.

2.4 Understanding Executive Functions and their Impairment in ADHD

Executive functions are cognitive processes that help individuals manage, regulate, and control their thoughts, actions, and behaviors. They play a crucial role in goal-directed behavior, decision-making, planning, problem-solving, working memory, cognitive flexibility, inhibitory control, and attentional allocation. Essentially, executive functions act as the "CEO" of the brain, overseeing and coordinating various mental processes to achieve desired outcomes.

In the context of Attention-Deficit/Hyperactivity Disorder (ADHD), there is often impairment in executive functions. ADHD is a neurodevelopmental disorder characterized by persistent patterns of inattention, hyperactivity, and impulsivity that can impact daily functioning and quality of life. While the exact causes of ADHD are complex and not fully understood, research suggests that genetic, environmental, and neurological factors contribute to its development.

Individuals with ADHD often exhibit difficulties in various aspects of executive functioning. In terms of working memory, they may struggle to hold and manipulate information for short periods, which can affect learning and problem-solving. Cognitive flexibility, the ability to switch between tasks or adapt to changing situations, might be compromised, leading to rigid thinking and difficulties with transitions. Inhibitory control deficits result in impulsive behaviors and difficulty inhibiting immediate responses in favor of more thoughtful ones.

Furthermore, individuals with ADHD frequently experience challenges with sustained attention, which is a key component of executive functions. They may struggle to maintain focus on tasks, get easily distracted, and have trouble organizing their activities. Planning and organization skills are often impaired, making it difficult to break down tasks into manageable steps and complete them in an organized manner.

Neuroimaging studies have shown that the prefrontal cortex, a brain region responsible for executive functions, tends to be underactive in individuals with ADHD. This supports the neurological basis for executive function impairments in this population.

It's important to note that executive function impairments in ADHD can vary in severity among individuals and may change over time. These difficulties can have a significant impact on academic performance, social interactions, occupational functioning, and overall well-being. However, it's also worth highlighting that individuals with ADHD often exhibit strengths in creativity, divergent thinking, and problem-solving under certain conditions.

Management of executive function impairments in ADHD typically involves a multimodal approach. This can include behavioral interventions, psychoeducation, cognitive-behavioral therapy, and, in some cases, medication. Tailoring interventions to individual strengths and challenges is essential for effective treatment.

In conclusion, executive functions are complex cognitive processes that facilitate goal-directed behavior, and their impairment in ADHD can lead to difficulties in attention, working memory, cognitive flexibility, inhibitory control, and planning. Understanding these challenges and implementing appropriate interventions can significantly improve the quality of life for individuals with ADHD.

Chapter 3

*Building a Supportive Environment:
Creating a Positive Home and School
Environment*

Creating a positive and supportive environment both at home and in school is essential for fostering growth, learning, and emotional well-being in individuals, particularly children. Such environments contribute significantly to overall development, academic success, and mental health. Here's an in-depth guide on building a supportive environment:

1. Clear Communication:

Encourage open and honest communication among family members and students.
Active listening promotes understanding and empathy.

At school, teachers should maintain clear communication channels with students, parents, and colleagues.

2. Establishing Trust:

Create an atmosphere where everyone feels safe and valued.

Demonstrate reliability and consistency in actions and decisions.

In schools, trust is built by treating students fairly, respecting their opinions, and maintaining confidentiality.

3. Positive Reinforcement:

Offer praise, encouragement, and constructive feedback.

Highlight strengths and accomplishments to boost self-esteem.

In a school setting, celebrate achievements, both big and small, to motivate students.

4. Setting Clear Expectations:

Define clear rules, boundaries, and expectations.

Establish routines to provide a sense of stability and predictability.

Schools should communicate academic and behavioral expectations to students and parents.

5. Emotional Support:

Show empathy and understanding during challenging times.

Encourage the expression of emotions and provide a safe space for processing feelings.

Schools can have counselors or support staff to assist students with emotional needs.

6. Promoting Growth Mindset:

Encourage a belief in the power of effort and the capacity to learn.

Emphasize that mistakes are opportunities for learning and growth.

Schools can cultivate a growth mindset through curriculum, discussions, and classroom activities.

7. Inclusive Environment:

Embrace diversity and create an environment free from discrimination.

Promote cultural understanding and sensitivity.

Schools should ensure inclusivity in curriculum, activities, and policies.

8. Healthy Relationships:

Model healthy relationships at home, fostering respect and cooperation.

At school, teach conflict resolution skills and promote peer collaboration.

9. Nurturing Curiosity:

Encourage curiosity, exploration, and a love for learning.
Provide access to books, educational resources, and hands-on experiences.
Schools can offer extracurricular activities to engage students' diverse interests.
10. Time Management and Balance:

Teach the importance of balancing responsibilities, activities, and leisure.
Help children and students prioritize tasks and manage time effectively.
11. Flexibility and Adaptability:

Embrace change as an opportunity for growth.
Adapt strategies to fit the evolving needs of individuals and situations.
12. Collaborative Efforts:

Involve family members, teachers, and students in decision-making processes.
Create partnerships between home and school to support holistic development.
Building a positive and supportive environment requires continuous effort, understanding, and dedication from both caregivers and educators. It's an

investment that yields lifelong benefits for individuals, contributing to their emotional well-being, academic success, and personal growth.

3.1 Establishing Routines and Structure in nurturing a child with adhd

Establishing routines and structure is crucial when nurturing a child with ADHD (Attention-Deficit/Hyperactivity Disorder). ADHD can lead to difficulties in managing time, focusing, and regulating emotions. Creating a consistent and organized environment helps the child develop essential skills and cope better with their challenges. Here's an in-depth guide on how to establish effective routines and structure:

Consistent Schedule: Maintain a consistent daily schedule with regular meal times, bedtime, and activities. Consistency helps the child anticipate what's coming next, reducing anxiety and impulsivity.

Visual Schedules: Use visual cues like charts, calendars, or timers to outline daily routines. Visual aids provide a tangible representation of time and tasks, aiding the child's understanding and preparation.

Prioritize Tasks: Break tasks into smaller, manageable steps. Teach the child to prioritize tasks and tackle them one at a time. This approach prevents them from feeling overwhelmed.

Set Clear Expectations: Clearly communicate rules and expectations for behavior. Use simple, specific language and positive reinforcement for following instructions.

Designated Spaces: Create designated spaces for specific activities, such as a quiet study area, a play area, and a calming corner. These spaces help the child transition between tasks and regulate their energy levels.

Transitions: ADHD children may struggle with transitions. Give them warnings before transitioning between activities and use visual cues to signal upcoming changes.

Regular Breaks: Integrate short, frequent breaks into their routine. These breaks help them refocus and recharge, preventing frustration and restlessness.

Consistent Sleep Routine: Ensure the child gets sufficient sleep by establishing a consistent bedtime routine. A good night's sleep can significantly improve focus and attention.

Morning Routine: Develop a structured morning routine to kickstart the day. Include activities like hygiene tasks, getting dressed, and having a nutritious breakfast.

Mealtime Routine: Maintain regular meal times and encourage healthy eating habits. Adequate nutrition can influence attention and behavior.

Homework Routine: Set a specific time for homework and create a quiet, organized workspace. Break down assignments into manageable chunks and use timers to help the child stay on track.

Physical Activity: Incorporate regular physical activities into the routine. Exercise can help manage excess energy and improve focus.

Rewards and Consequences: Implement a system of rewards for completing tasks and following routines. Also, establish consistent consequences for not adhering to rules, helping the child understand the importance of structure.

Flexibility: While routines are important, allow some flexibility to accommodate unforeseen circumstances. Teach the child how to adapt to changes without becoming overly anxious.

Parental Self-Care: Nurturing a child with ADHD can be challenging, so ensure you take care of yourself. Your well-being influences your ability to provide structure and support.

Remember that every child is unique, and it may take time to find the routines and strategies that work best for them. Regular communication with teachers, therapists, and healthcare professionals can provide additional insights and guidance tailored to the child's needs.

3.2 Setting Clear Expectations and Boundaries

Setting clear expectations and boundaries is a crucial aspect of effective communication and maintaining healthy relationships, whether in personal or professional contexts. It involves establishing guidelines, limits, and anticipated outcomes to ensure mutual understanding and respect among individuals involved. Here's an in-depth look at the importance and strategies for setting clear expectations and boundaries:

Importance of Setting Clear Expectations:

Prevention of Misunderstandings: Clear expectations minimize the likelihood of misunderstandings, conflicts, and disappointments. When everyone is on the same page about goals, responsibilities, and outcomes, it reduces confusion and frustration.

Enhanced Accountability: Well-defined expectations create accountability as individuals know what is expected of them. This increases their sense of ownership and commitment towards meeting those expectations.

Improved Performance: When people know exactly what is required, they can focus their efforts on delivering results. This can lead to improved performance and productivity, benefiting both individuals and organizations.

Positive Relationships: Clear expectations foster positive relationships by building trust and reducing uncertainty. People feel valued when their roles and responsibilities are well-communicated.

Strategies for Setting Clear Expectations and Boundaries:

Open Communication: Begin by engaging in open and transparent discussions. Clearly articulate your needs, goals, and requirements while encouraging others to do the same. Address any questions or concerns to ensure everyone has a shared understanding.

Be Specific: Avoid vague language. Clearly define what is expected, including the scope of work, deadlines, quality standards, and any other relevant details. Ambiguity can lead to confusion.

Mutual Agreement: Whenever possible, involve all parties in defining expectations. This collaborative approach ensures that expectations are realistic and feasible for everyone involved.

Document Expectations: Put expectations in writing, such as emails, project briefs, or contracts. Having a written record serves as a reference point and minimizes the chances of memory-based disputes.

Regular Check-Ins: Establish a mechanism for regular check-ins to assess progress and address any concerns. This maintains alignment and allows for adjustments if necessary.

Flexibility: While clear boundaries are important, be open to some flexibility. Situations may change, and being rigid can hinder collaboration. Assess changes within the context of the established boundaries.

Respect Individual Limits: Recognize that everyone has different capacities and limits. Be mindful of personal boundaries to avoid overloading individuals or creating an unsustainable work environment.

Lead by Example: If you're in a leadership role, demonstrate adherence to boundaries and expectations. This sets a precedent for others to follow.

Handle Violations Appropriately: If someone crosses a boundary or fails to meet an expectation, address the situation promptly and respectfully. Use it as an opportunity to reaffirm the importance of the established guidelines.

In conclusion, setting clear expectations and boundaries is a cornerstone of effective communication, collaboration, and healthy relationships. It promotes understanding, accountability, and a positive atmosphere, ultimately contributing to successful outcomes in various aspects of life.

3.3 Promoting Effective Communication with Your Child and School

Promoting effective communication between parents, children, and schools is crucial for fostering a supportive and enriching educational experience. Here's an in-depth look at strategies to achieve this:

Open Channels of Communication:
Establish clear lines of communication with your child's school. Attend parent-teacher conferences, back-to-school nights, and other school events to interact with teachers, administrators, and other parents. This initial connection can form the basis for ongoing communication.

Active Listening:
When your child talks about their school day, be an attentive listener. Encourage them to share their thoughts, concerns, and achievements. This shows

them that you value their experiences and helps build trust.

Regular Check-ins:
Regularly check in with your child about their school life. Ask about their assignments, projects, and any challenges they're facing. Regular conversations help you stay informed and offer guidance when needed.

Establish a Routine:
Set a routine for discussing school matters. This could be during family meals or designated "homework time." A consistent schedule makes it easier for your child to share their experiences.

Use of Technology:
Utilize digital platforms or apps provided by the school to stay updated on assignments, grades, and school announcements. These tools facilitate seamless communication between parents and teachers.

Respectful Interaction:
Maintain a respectful tone when communicating with school staff. Whether in-person, via email, or during meetings, maintaining professionalism fosters a positive relationship.

Participate in School Activities:
Attend school events, volunteer opportunities, and workshops. Involvement demonstrates your commitment to your child's education and allows you to engage with the school community.

Collaborative Problem-Solving:
If issues arise, collaborate with teachers and administrators to find solutions. Approach concerns with an open mind, seeking to understand different perspectives and working together to address challenges.

Regular Updates with Teachers:
Stay in touch with teachers regarding your child's progress. Inquire about strengths and areas needing improvement. This partnership ensures you're aware of your child's academic journey.

Provide Feedback:
Offer constructive feedback to the school when appropriate. Share insights about what's working well and areas that might need improvement. Schools value parental input to enhance their programs.

Support Homework and Learning:
Create a conducive environment at home for learning. Provide a quiet space for homework, and be

available for assistance when needed. Encourage independent work while being there to guide when necessary.

Celebrate Achievements:
Acknowledge and celebrate your child's achievements, both big and small. This positivity reinforces their efforts and motivates them to continue excelling.

Remember, effective communication is a two-way street. By actively engaging with your child's school and maintaining open lines of communication, you create a collaborative and supportive environment that contributes to your child's overall growth and success.

3.4 Collaborating with Teachers and Educators to Support your Child's Needs

Collaborating with teachers and educators is crucial to effectively support your child's educational needs. Communication and partnership between parents and educators can create a positive learning environment tailored to your child's requirements.

Here's an in-depth look at how to collaborate effectively:

Open Communication: Initiate open and regular communication with teachers. Share information about your child's strengths, weaknesses, learning styles, and any challenges they may face. Likewise, teachers should update you on your child's progress, behavior, and areas needing improvement.

Set Clear Goals: Define specific goals for your child's education. These could relate to academic achievements, social skills, or personal development. Collaboratively, create a plan to achieve these goals, taking into consideration both home and school environments.

Individualized Education Plan (IEP): For children with special needs, develop an IEP. This legal document outlines the educational goals, required support, and necessary accommodations. Regularly review and update the IEP to ensure your child's progress.

Attend Parent-Teacher Conferences: Participate actively in parent-teacher conferences. Discuss your child's academic performance, behavior, and any concerns you or the teacher might have.

Collaboratively brainstorm strategies to address challenges and build on strengths.

Share Resources: Both parents and teachers can share resources, such as educational materials, websites, or strategies that have worked well. This exchange of ideas can enhance the learning experience for the child.

Consistent Routine: Establish a consistent routine that includes study time, homework, playtime, and rest. Communicate this routine to teachers so they can align their expectations and assignments accordingly.

Volunteer and Participate: Participate in school activities, events, and volunteering opportunities. This involvement demonstrates your commitment to your child's education and helps you build relationships with educators.

Problem-Solving Approach: Approach challenges as a team. If your child is struggling academically or socially, collaborate with teachers to identify the root causes and brainstorm solutions together.

Recognize and Appreciate: Acknowledge the efforts of teachers in supporting your child's learning journey. Express gratitude for their dedication and hard work.

Stay Informed: Keep up-to-date with the curriculum, school policies, and educational trends. This knowledge enables you to engage more effectively in conversations with teachers.

Respect Professional Expertise: While you know your child best, remember that teachers have professional expertise in education. Be open to their suggestions and recommendations.

Technology and Apps: Utilize educational technology and apps recommended by teachers to enhance learning outside of school hours.

Positive Feedback Loop: Provide feedback to teachers about what's working well at home and how the child is responding to different strategies. This feedback loop strengthens the collaboration.

Conflict Resolution: If conflicts arise, address them calmly and respectfully. Misunderstandings can be resolved through open dialogue and a shared commitment to your child's well-being.

Remember, the ultimate goal of collaborating with teachers and educators is to create a cohesive, supportive learning environment that nurtures your child's growth and development.

Chapter 4

Nurturing Emotional Well-being: Managing Emotions and Promoting Resilience

Nurturing emotional well-being involves actively managing emotions and promoting resilience. Emotions play a vital role in our lives, influencing thoughts, behaviors, and overall mental health. Effective emotional management involves recognizing, understanding, and appropriately responding to these emotions.

Self-Awareness: Developing emotional intelligence begins with self-awareness. This involves recognizing and acknowledging your emotions without judgment. Mindfulness practices, like meditation, can help in cultivating this awareness.

Emotion Regulation: Once emotions are identified, it's important to regulate them. Strategies include deep breathing, progressive muscle relaxation, and reframing negative thoughts. These techniques enable individuals to manage emotional intensity and avoid impulsive reactions.

Coping Skills: Building a toolkit of healthy coping mechanisms is crucial. Engaging in activities you enjoy, seeking social support, and practicing stress-reduction techniques are ways to manage emotional challenges effectively.

Social Connections: Human connections are integral to emotional well-being. Strong social support networks provide opportunities for expression, validation, and comfort during tough times.

Resilience Building: Resilience is the ability to bounce back from adversity. Cultivating resilience involves developing problem-solving skills, adapting to change, and maintaining a positive outlook.

Positive Psychology: Focusing on positive experiences and emotions can enhance overall well-being. Practicing gratitude, engaging in acts of kindness, and savoring enjoyable moments contribute to a positive mindset.

Healthy Lifestyle: Physical health is interconnected with emotional well-being. Regular exercise, balanced nutrition, and adequate sleep positively impact mood and resilience.

Professional Help: Sometimes, emotions become overwhelming, and seeking therapy or counseling can provide valuable guidance. Therapists offer techniques to address deep-rooted emotional challenges.

Emotional Expression: Allowing yourself to express emotions in a healthy manner prevents emotional suppression. Writing in journals, engaging in art, or engaging in creative activities can serve as outlets.

Mindset Shifts: Challenging negative thought patterns and replacing them with more balanced perspectives is essential. Cognitive-behavioral therapy (CBT) is an evidence-based approach for fostering such shifts.

In summary, nurturing emotional well-being is a holistic process involving self-awareness, effective emotion regulation, coping skills, strong social connections, resilience building, positive psychology practices, a healthy lifestyle, seeking professional help when needed, emotional expression, and promoting positive mindset shifts. Regular practice of these strategies contributes to enhanced emotional well-being and overall life satisfaction.

4.1 Understanding Emotional Regulation in Children with ADHD

Emotional regulation in children with Attention-Deficit/Hyperactivity Disorder (ADHD) is a complex and critical aspect of their psychological well-being and overall functioning. This article delves into a comprehensive understanding of emotional regulation challenges faced by children with ADHD, exploring its underlying mechanisms, associated factors, and potential interventions.

1. Emotional Dysregulation in ADHD:
Children with ADHD often struggle with managing their emotions effectively. They may exhibit impulsive behavior, difficulty controlling emotional responses, and experience intense emotional outbursts. This dysregulation can impact their relationships, academic performance, and overall quality of life.

2. Underlying Mechanisms:

Neurologically, ADHD is linked to deficiencies in areas of the brain responsible for executive functions, including emotional regulation. The prefrontal cortex, responsible for impulse control and emotional modulation, is often underactive in children with ADHD. Dopamine dysregulation, a hallmark of ADHD, further influences emotional responses and self-control.

3. Factors Influencing Emotional Regulation:
Several factors contribute to emotional dysregulation in children with ADHD. These include genetics, environmental factors, family dynamics, comorbidities (such as anxiety or oppositional defiant disorder), and even the child's temperament. Additionally, the demands of school, social interactions, and the need to adhere to rules and routines can further challenge their emotional regulation abilities.

4. Impact on Social Interactions:
Emotional dysregulation can strain relationships, as children with ADHD may struggle to interpret social cues and respond appropriately. Their impulsive behavior and emotional outbursts might lead to peer rejection and feelings of isolation. Over time, this can erode self-esteem and exacerbate emotional difficulties.

5. Interventions and Strategies:
a. Psychoeducation: Providing children, parents, and teachers with information about ADHD and its impact on emotional regulation can foster understanding and empathy.
b. Cognitive-Behavioral Therapy (CBT): CBT techniques can help children recognize and challenge irrational thoughts, develop coping strategies, and enhance emotional awareness.
c. Mindfulness and Relaxation Techniques: These techniques can improve emotional self-regulation by teaching children to manage stress and cultivate present-moment awareness.
d. Medication: In some cases, stimulant medications may be prescribed to address core symptoms of ADHD, which can indirectly impact emotional regulation.

6. Parental and Educational Support:
Parents and educators play a crucial role in helping children with ADHD manage their emotions. Creating structured routines, setting clear expectations, and implementing consistent consequences for behavior can provide a sense of predictability and security, aiding emotional regulation.

7. Multimodal Approach:

A holistic approach that combines various interventions is often most effective. This might involve a combination of therapy, medication (if deemed appropriate by a medical professional), school accommodations, and ongoing support from parents and educators.

In conclusion, understanding emotional regulation in children with ADHD requires a multidimensional perspective. Addressing the underlying neurological and psychological factors, while implementing tailored interventions, can empower these children to navigate their emotions more effectively, leading to improved social relationships, academic success, and overall well-being.

4.2 Teaching Coping Strategies for Emotional Challenges

Teaching coping strategies for emotional challenges involves equipping individuals with practical tools to manage and navigate difficult emotions. These strategies can be divided into various categories:

Mindfulness and Relaxation Techniques: Mindfulness practices, deep breathing exercises, meditation, and progressive muscle relaxation help individuals stay present and manage stress.

Cognitive Restructuring: This involves identifying and challenging negative thought patterns that contribute to emotional distress. Encouraging individuals to reframe their thoughts in a more balanced and positive way can lead to improved emotional well-being.

Problem-Solving Skills: Teaching individuals how to analyze problems, break them down into manageable parts, and generate effective solutions can empower them to tackle challenges more effectively.

Emotion Regulation Skills: Understanding and managing emotions is key. Techniques such as recognizing triggers, practicing emotional acceptance, and utilizing positive self-talk can be valuable tools.

Social Support and Communication: Encouraging open communication and fostering healthy relationships can provide a support system when facing emotional difficulties.

Physical Well-being: Highlighting the importance of regular exercise, balanced nutrition, and adequate sleep can significantly impact emotional resilience.

Engaging in Activities: Encouraging individuals to pursue hobbies, interests, and activities they enjoy can be an effective way to redirect focus from negative emotions.

Time Management: Teaching effective time management skills can prevent feelings of overwhelm and stress, promoting a sense of control over one's life.

Assertiveness Training: Helping individuals communicate their needs and boundaries confidently can reduce feelings of powerlessness and improve self-esteem.

Journaling: Writing down thoughts and emotions can provide an outlet for processing feelings and gaining insights into personal patterns.

Seeking Professional Help: Educating individuals about the importance of seeking therapy or counseling when needed can destigmatize mental health support.

When teaching coping strategies, it's important to tailor the approach to individual preferences and needs. Combining these strategies can create a comprehensive toolkit for effectively managing emotional challenges and promoting overall well-being.

4.3 Promoting Self-esteem and Confidence in Children with ADHD

Promoting self-esteem and confidence in children with ADHD is a crucial aspect of their overall development. ADHD (Attention-Deficit/Hyperactivity Disorder) can often lead to challenges in academic performance, social interactions, and emotional well-being. Here are some in-depth strategies to foster self-esteem and confidence in these children:

Emphasize Strengths: Focus on identifying and nurturing the child's strengths and interests. Recognizing their talents and achievements, even in small tasks, helps boost their self-worth.

Set Realistic Goals: Work together with the child to set achievable goals, both academically and behaviorally. These goals should be specific, measurable, and time-bound, helping the child experience a sense of accomplishment.

Provide Structured Environment: Children with ADHD often benefit from a structured routine. Consistent schedules and clear expectations provide a sense of security and control, enhancing their confidence in managing daily tasks.

Break Tasks into Manageable Steps: Large tasks can be overwhelming for children with ADHD. Breaking them down into smaller, manageable steps makes them feel less daunting and more achievable.

Celebrate Progress: Regularly acknowledge and celebrate the child's progress. Positive reinforcement through praise and rewards reinforces their self-esteem and motivation.

Encourage Self-Advocacy: Teach the child to communicate their needs, preferences, and challenges. This empowers them to seek help when needed, promoting self-advocacy and self-confidence.

Provide Immediate Feedback: Immediate feedback helps children with ADHD connect actions to consequences. Constructive feedback should focus on behavior rather than the child's character.

Teach Coping Strategies: Equip the child with coping strategies for managing impulsivity, attention difficulties, and frustration. These strategies empower them to navigate challenges effectively.

Social Skills Training: Social interactions can be challenging for children with ADHD. Social skills training can help them develop the tools needed for successful interactions and positive relationships.

Promote Mindfulness and Self-Awareness: Mindfulness practices help children become more aware of their thoughts, emotions, and behaviors. This self-awareness fosters better self-regulation and emotional well-being.

Provide Peer Support: Encourage the child to engage in group activities or support groups with peers who may have similar challenges. This provides a sense of belonging and normalizes their experiences.

Involve the Family: Collaboration between parents, teachers, and healthcare professionals is crucial. A united approach ensures consistent strategies and support both at home and in school.

Address Negative Self-Talk: Children with ADHD may develop negative self-perceptions due to challenges they face. Help them challenge and reframe negative thoughts to build a healthier self-image.

Foster Independence: Gradually encourage the child to take on more responsibilities and make decisions. Developing a sense of independence positively impacts their self-esteem.

Model Self-Compassion: Be a role model by demonstrating self-compassion and acceptance of mistakes. This encourages the child to develop a forgiving attitude towards themselves.

Every child with ADHD is unique, and the strategies that work best may vary. Consistent support, patience, and understanding are key components in promoting self-esteem and confidence in these children. It's important to tailor interventions based on the child's individual needs and strengths. If you're seeking professional advice, consulting with a qualified mental health professional or therapist experienced in working with ADHD can provide personalized guidance.

4.4 Addressing Co-occurring Mental Health Conditions in Children with ADHD

Addressing co-occurring mental health conditions in children with Attention-Deficit/Hyperactivity Disorder (ADHD) is a complex and crucial aspect of providing comprehensive care. Co-occurring conditions, also referred to as comorbidities, often present significant challenges as they can exacerbate the symptoms of ADHD and impact the overall well-being of the child. This in-depth discussion will delve into the various co-occurring mental health conditions commonly observed in children with ADHD and strategies for their effective management.

1. Common Co-occurring Conditions:
Children with ADHD frequently experience co-occurring mental health conditions such as:

Oppositional Defiant Disorder (ODD): This condition is characterized by defiant and hostile behavior, often manifesting as frequent temper outbursts, argumentativeness, and defiance toward authority figures.

Conduct Disorder (CD): CD involves more severe behavioral problems, including aggression, vandalism, and violation of others' rights. It often begins as ODD and can escalate into more serious conduct issues.

Anxiety Disorders: Conditions like Generalized Anxiety Disorder, Social Anxiety Disorder, and Specific Phobias are commonly seen alongside ADHD. Anxiety can intensify ADHD symptoms and hinder daily functioning.

Depressive Disorders: Children with ADHD are at a higher risk of experiencing depression. Symptoms may include persistent sadness, loss of interest, fatigue, and changes in sleep and appetite.

2. Challenges in Diagnosis:
Diagnosing co-occurring conditions can be complex due to the overlapping symptoms with ADHD. Additionally, children with ADHD might struggle to express their emotions and experiences accurately.

3. Holistic Approach to Treatment:
Managing co-occurring conditions involves a comprehensive approach that considers both ADHD and the accompanying mental health issues. Strategies include:

Accurate Diagnosis: Thorough evaluation by mental health professionals is crucial to identify co-occurring conditions accurately.

Behavioral Therapy: Interventions like Cognitive Behavioral Therapy (CBT) can help address anxiety, depression, and conduct issues by teaching coping skills and promoting positive behaviors.

Medication Management: Depending on the severity of symptoms, medication might be prescribed to address specific conditions such as anxiety or depression. However, it should be used judiciously and monitored closely.

Parent Training: Providing parents with effective parenting strategies can help manage disruptive behaviors and improve family dynamics.

School Support: Collaborating with teachers and school staff to implement Individualized Education Plans (IEPs) or 504 Plans can aid in addressing academic and behavioral challenges.

Support Groups: Both children and parents can benefit from participating in support groups that offer a safe space to share experiences and learn from others facing similar challenges.

4. Long-Term Outlook:
Addressing co-occurring conditions early on can have a positive impact on a child's development. Effective management not only improves their immediate quality of life but also reduces the risk of these issues persisting into adulthood.

In conclusion, addressing co-occurring mental health conditions in children with ADHD requires a multifaceted and individualized approach. By recognizing the presence of these conditions, seeking proper diagnosis, and implementing a comprehensive treatment plan, we can help children with ADHD lead more fulfilling and successful lives while managing their co-occurring challenges. Always consult with qualified healthcare professionals for accurate diagnosis and personalized treatment recommendations.

Chapter 5

Developing Effective Parenting Strategies: Techniques for Managing Behavior

Developing effective parenting strategies requires a thoughtful and balanced approach. Here are some techniques for managing behavior in children:

Positive Reinforcement: Rewarding desired behaviors can encourage their repetition. Offer praise, privileges, or small treats when your child displays good behavior, reinforcing their positive actions.

Clear Communication: Clearly convey your expectations and rules to your child. Use simple language and be consistent in your messaging. This helps reduce misunderstandings and sets a clear framework for behavior.

Set Realistic Expectations: Understand your child's developmental stage and set age-appropriate expectations. Unrealistic demands can lead to frustration for both you and your child.

Consistency: Consistency is key to effective parenting. Apply rules and consequences consistently so that your child knows what to expect. This fosters a sense of stability and predictability.

Time-Outs: When a child misbehaves, a brief time-out can help them calm down and reflect on their actions. Use this as an opportunity to discuss their behavior once they've cooled off.

Model Behavior: Children often learn by observing their parents. Display the behavior you want them to emulate, whether it's practicing patience, respectful communication, or emotional regulation.

Limit-Setting: Establish clear limits and boundaries. Children feel more secure when they know what is acceptable and what isn't. Be firm but empathetic when enforcing these boundaries.

Problem-Solving Discussions: Instead of immediately resorting to punishment, engage in problem-solving discussions. Help your child understand the consequences of their actions and involve them in finding solutions.

Natural Consequences: Allow children to experience the natural consequences of their actions, within reason. This helps them learn from their mistakes and take responsibility for their choices.

Use of Privileges: Connect privileges to responsible behavior. If your child fulfills certain responsibilities, they earn the privilege of participating in preferred activities.

Avoid Power Struggles: Choose your battles wisely. Sometimes, it's better to let minor issues slide to avoid unnecessary power struggles. Focus on addressing more significant behavioral concerns.

Empathy and Validation: When your child is upset, show empathy and validate their feelings. This can help them feel understood and reduce the likelihood of negative behavior.

Time and Attention: Spend quality time with your child. Providing positive attention can prevent them from seeking negative attention through misbehavior.

Routine and Structure: Children thrive on routine and structure. A consistent daily routine can help minimize disruptions and promote positive behavior.

Educate Yourself: Stay informed about child development and effective parenting techniques. Books, articles, and parenting courses can provide valuable insights.

Remember that every child is unique, so it's important to tailor your parenting strategies to their individual personality and needs. Flexibility, patience, and open communication are key elements of successful parenting.

5.1 Positive Reinforcement and Reward Systems for adhd

Positive reinforcement and reward systems are effective strategies for managing ADHD (Attention Deficit Hyperactivity Disorder) symptoms and improving behavior. These strategies are based on behavioral psychology principles and involve providing rewards or incentives to encourage desired behaviors and discourage unwanted ones.

Understanding Positive Reinforcement:

Positive reinforcement involves presenting a reward immediately after a desired behavior is exhibited, making it more likely for that behavior to be repeated in the future. In the context of ADHD, this could be used to reinforce tasks like completing homework, staying focused, following instructions, or managing impulsivity.

Choosing Appropriate Rewards:
Rewards should be chosen based on individual preferences and interests. They can range from tangible rewards like small toys, stickers, or privileges, to intangible rewards like extra screen time, a favorite activity, or verbal praise. Tailoring rewards to the individual's preferences increases the effectiveness of the strategy.

Consistency and Timeliness:
For positive reinforcement to be effective, rewards need to be delivered consistently and promptly after the desired behavior is exhibited. This helps establish a clear connection between the behavior and the reward, reinforcing the behavior's occurrence.

Setting Clear Goals:
Setting achievable goals is essential. Start with small, attainable tasks and gradually increase the

complexity of tasks as the individual improves. This prevents frustration and maintains motivation.

Using Token Systems:
Token systems involve earning tokens or points for each appropriate behavior displayed. These tokens can be exchanged for a larger reward once a certain number is accumulated. Token systems can be particularly effective for complex tasks that need to be broken down into smaller steps.

Combining Immediate and Delayed Rewards:
While immediate rewards work well for short-term tasks, delayed rewards can be effective for teaching patience and perseverance. For instance, a larger reward can be promised for maintaining good behavior over a longer period.

Involvement and Collaboration:
Incorporate the individual's input when designing the reward system. This fosters a sense of ownership and motivation. Additionally, involving parents, teachers, or caregivers ensures consistency across different settings.

Regular Assessment and Adaptation:
Monitor the effectiveness of the reward system over time. If certain behaviors are not responding to the

chosen rewards, it might be necessary to adjust the incentives. Flexibility is key to finding what works best for each individual.

Gradual Fading:
As behaviors improve, gradually reduce the frequency or magnitude of rewards. The goal is to eventually have the individual engage in desired behaviors without needing external rewards.

Balancing with Consequences:
While positive reinforcement is crucial, it's important to address negative behaviors with appropriate consequences. Consistently ignoring unwanted behaviors can reinforce them inadvertently.

Remember that every individual with ADHD is unique, so it might take some trial and error to find the most effective combination of rewards and strategies. Consulting with a mental health professional, such as a therapist or psychiatrist, can provide personalized guidance and support in implementing these techniques.

5.2 Implementing Consistent Discipline Strategies

Implementing consistent discipline strategies is crucial for maintaining a positive and structured environment for individuals, whether it's in a family, educational, or professional setting. Consistency in discipline helps establish clear expectations, promote behavioral development, and foster a sense of fairness. Here's an in-depth guide to effectively implement consistent discipline strategies:

Define Clear Expectations:
Clearly communicate the rules, expectations, and consequences to all parties involved. Make sure the rules are age-appropriate, realistic, and well-understood. Having a written code of conduct can serve as a reference point.

Lead by Example:
Role modeling is essential. Demonstrate the behaviors and attitudes you expect from others. Consistent discipline starts with adults showing the desired behaviors themselves.

Establish Consequences:

Set appropriate consequences for both positive and negative behaviors. Consequences should be logical and related to the behavior. Consistency means that similar behaviors will result in similar consequences each time.

Use Positive Reinforcement:
Acknowledge and reward good behavior to encourage its repetition. This can be in the form of praise, tokens, privileges, or small rewards. Positive reinforcement can be more effective than solely focusing on negative consequences.

Stay Calm and Controlled:
When addressing misbehavior, remain composed. Avoid reacting impulsively out of frustration. A calm demeanor will help you enforce discipline more effectively.

Address Behavior, Not Person:
Focus on addressing the specific behavior that needs correction, rather than attacking the individual's character. This approach is less likely to lead to defensiveness and more likely to promote understanding.

Communicate Clearly:

Explain the reasons behind the rules and consequences. Encourage open communication where the individual can express their thoughts and concerns, fostering understanding and compliance.

Be Predictable:
Maintain consistency in applying consequences. When individuals know what to expect, they are more likely to modify their behavior to align with expectations.

Collaborative Approach:
In family or educational settings, involve everyone affected by the discipline strategy in discussions about rules and consequences. This shared decision-making can increase ownership and commitment.

Reevaluate and Adjust:
Periodically review the effectiveness of your discipline strategies. Be willing to make adjustments based on changing circumstances, individual progress, and feedback.

Long-Term Perspective:
Recognize that consistent discipline is a process that requires time. Aim for gradual improvement rather than immediate perfection.

Empathy and Understanding:
Remember that individuals might have various reasons for their behavior. Show empathy and understanding while addressing misbehavior, helping individuals learn from their mistakes.

Document and Track:
Keep records of behaviors, consequences, and improvements over time. This can help you monitor progress and adjust strategies as needed.

Involve Everyone:
In shared environments, such as classrooms or workplaces, ensure that everyone responsible for implementing discipline strategies is on the same page. Consistency across all adults is crucial.

Continuous Learning:
Stay informed about effective discipline techniques and psychological principles. Continuous learning can enhance your ability to implement consistent discipline strategies.

Remember, the goal of consistent discipline is not just to correct behavior but to guide individuals toward responsible, ethical, and respectful conduct. It requires patience, dedication, and a commitment to the well-being and growth of those involved.

5.3 Utilizing Behavior Modification Techniques

Behavior modification techniques are a set of psychological interventions that aim to alter or influence individuals' behaviors through systematic and structured approaches. These techniques are commonly used in various settings, such as clinical therapy, education, and organizational management, to bring about positive changes in behavior. Let's delve into some of the key aspects of utilizing behavior modification techniques:

Identifying Target Behaviors: The first step in behavior modification is to identify the specific behavior that needs to be modified. This behavior should be observable, measurable, and defined clearly. For example, if the target behavior is to reduce procrastination, the behavior can be defined as starting a task within 10 minutes of planning.

Setting Clear Goals: Behavior modification involves setting clear and realistic goals. Goals provide direction and a sense of accomplishment. Goals should be specific, measurable, achievable, relevant, and time-bound (SMART). Using the procrastination example, a goal could be to start a task within 10 minutes at least four days a week.

Positive Reinforcement: Positive reinforcement involves rewarding desired behaviors to increase the likelihood of their recurrence. Rewards can be tangible (e.g., treats, prizes) or intangible (e.g., praise, recognition). If an individual starts a task within the designated time frame, they might reward themselves with a short break or a favorite snack.

Negative Reinforcement: Negative reinforcement is about removing or avoiding something unpleasant to encourage the desired behavior. For instance, if someone completes a chore promptly, they might avoid the stress of rushing later. Negative reinforcement is not the same as punishment, as it focuses on creating positive outcomes.

Punishment: Punishment is the introduction of an undesirable consequence to decrease the likelihood of a behavior occurring again. While it can be effective in some cases, it should be used cautiously, as it can lead to negative emotions and unintended consequences. It's generally recommended to prioritize positive reinforcement over punishment.

Extinction: Extinction involves withholding rewards or attention previously associated with a behavior. This approach is used when a behavior is no longer desired. For example, if a child throws tantrums for attention, ignoring the tantrums can lead to their gradual decrease.

Behavioral Contracts: Behavioral contracts are written agreements between individuals outlining the expected behaviors and the rewards or consequences associated with them. These contracts provide clarity and accountability, making behavior modification more structured and effective.

Self-Monitoring: Self-monitoring involves keeping track of one's own behaviors and progress toward goals. This can be done through journals, apps, or other tools. It enhances self-awareness and helps individuals stay on track.

Cognitive-Behavioral   Techniques: Cognitive-behavioral techniques focus on identifying and altering negative thought patterns that contribute to undesired behaviors. By changing thought patterns, individuals can change their responses and behaviors.

Social Support: Engaging friends, family, or support groups can provide encouragement and accountability during behavior modification efforts. Positive social interactions can reinforce desired behaviors.

Gradual Progression: Behavior modification often works best when changes are implemented gradually. Sudden, drastic changes can be overwhelming and difficult to maintain.

Remember that the effectiveness of behavior modification techniques varies from person to person. It's important to consider individual preferences, motivations, and potential underlying factors that might influence behavior. Consulting with a trained professional, such as a psychologist or behavior analyst, can provide personalized guidance and ensure the best approach for achieving the desired behavioral changes.

5.4 Addressing Hyperactivity and Impulsivity

Addressing hyperactivity and impulsivity involves a comprehensive approach that encompasses various strategies and interventions. These challenges are often associated with conditions like Attention-Deficit/Hyperactivity Disorder (ADHD), but they can also be present in other contexts. Here's an in-depth look at addressing these issues:

Behavioral Interventions: Behavioral therapies, such as Cognitive Behavioral Therapy (CBT) and behavior modification, can help individuals learn to recognize impulsive behaviors and develop strategies to manage them. These interventions often involve setting goals, monitoring behavior, and using rewards or consequences to reinforce positive changes.

Parent and Caregiver Training: For children, involving parents and caregivers is crucial. Providing them with tools to manage hyperactivity and impulsivity at home and in various settings can significantly improve a child's behavior. This includes teaching techniques to set clear expectations, establish routines, and use effective discipline strategies.

Medication: In cases of diagnosed ADHD, medication might be considered. Stimulant medications like methylphenidate and amphetamine-based drugs are commonly prescribed to manage symptoms of hyperactivity and impulsivity. Non-stimulant medications like atomoxetine might also be used.

Educational Support: In educational settings, teachers can play a pivotal role. Tailoring classroom environments to accommodate the needs of students with hyperactivity and impulsivity, such as providing frequent breaks, minimizing distractions, and using visual aids, can improve their focus and engagement.

Mindfulness and Relaxation Techniques: Teaching individuals relaxation strategies and mindfulness techniques can enhance their ability to manage impulsive behaviors. Techniques like deep breathing, meditation, and progressive muscle relaxation can help individuals pause and respond thoughtfully to situations.

Physical Activity: Regular physical exercise can be beneficial in reducing hyperactivity. Engaging in activities that require focus and self-regulation, such as yoga or martial arts, can help channel excess energy and teach self-control.

Time Management Skills: Teaching individuals effective time management skills can aid in planning tasks, setting priorities, and avoiding impulsive decisions. Using tools like timers, schedules, and to-do lists can improve organization and structure.

Social Skills Training: Impulsivity can impact social interactions. Social skills training can teach individuals how to navigate social situations, including waiting their turn, listening actively, and considering the consequences of their actions on others.

Environmental Modifications: Creating an environment that minimizes triggers for impulsive behavior is important. This might involve reducing clutter, creating designated workspaces, and minimizing distractions.

Individualized Approach: Recognize that each individual is unique. Tailor interventions to suit their specific needs, strengths, and challenges. Regular monitoring and adjustments to strategies may be necessary.

It's important to remember that addressing hyperactivity and impulsivity requires patience and consistency. A multidisciplinary approach involving mental health professionals, educators, parents, and caregivers can provide the best outcomes for individuals struggling with these challenges. If you're dealing with these issues personally or with someone you know, seeking guidance from qualified professionals is highly recommended.

Chapter 6

Enhancing Academic Success: Strategies for Learning and Studying

Enhancing academic success involves effective strategies such as active learning, time management, setting goals, taking breaks, and seeking help when needed

Here are some strategies that can help enhance academic success for a child with ADHD:

Structured Routine: Establish a consistent daily routine with designated study times, breaks, meals, and sleep. Predictability can help the child stay focused and manage their time effectively.

Organizational Tools: Use tools like planners, calendars, and color-coded folders to help the child keep track of assignments, projects, and deadlines.

Visual Aids: Utilize visual aids such as charts, diagrams, and mind maps to present information in a more engaging and comprehensible manner.

Short Study Sessions: Break down studying into shorter, focused sessions. Use techniques like the Pomodoro Technique, with periods of intense concentration followed by short breaks.

Active Learning: Incorporate interactive methods like hands-on activities, group discussions, or teaching the material to someone else to enhance engagement and understanding.

Multisensory Learning: Encourage learning through multiple senses by incorporating visuals, auditory cues, and tactile experiences.

Chunking Information: Divide information into smaller chunks and provide regular reviews to reinforce learning and retention.

Quiet Study Environment: Create a quiet and organized study space to minimize distractions and help the child concentrate better.

Use of Technology: Leverage educational apps, online tools, and digital resources designed to aid learning and attention.

Positive Reinforcement: Provide praise and rewards for completing tasks and achieving milestones, fostering a sense of accomplishment.

Clear Instructions: Break down assignments into clear and manageable steps. Use visual or written instructions to help the child understand expectations.

Incorporate Movement: Allow for short movement breaks during study sessions to help the child release excess energy and refocus.

Self-Monitoring: Teach the child self-monitoring techniques, such as checking their work for errors and evaluating their own progress.

Goal Setting: Set achievable short-term and long-term goals with the child, helping them track their progress and stay motivated.

Regular Communication: Maintain open communication with teachers and educators to collaborate on strategies that support the child's learning needs.

Remember that each child is unique, so it's essential to tailor these strategies to fit the child's preferences and strengths. Additionally, working closely with educators, specialists, and medical professionals can help create a comprehensive approach to support the child's academic success.

6.1 Creating an Optimal Learning Environment at Home for your adhd child

Creating an optimal learning environment at home for a child with ADHD requires careful consideration of various factors. Here's an in-depth guide to help you establish a conducive setting for their learning and development:

Designated Workspace: Set up a dedicated and clutter-free workspace for your child. This area should be free from distractions and have all the necessary learning materials easily accessible.

Organization: Use storage solutions like shelves, bins, and organizers to keep school supplies, books, and learning tools neatly arranged. This promotes a sense of order and reduces distractions.

Visual Structure: Incorporate visual cues such as color-coded folders, calendars, and schedules to help your child understand their daily routines and tasks.

Minimal Distractions: Choose a quiet and well-lit space away from high-traffic areas, TVs, and noisy appliances. Consider noise-canceling headphones if noise remains an issue.

Flexible Seating: Allow for flexible seating options like a comfortable chair or a standing desk. Some children with ADHD find it easier to focus when they can move around a bit.

Personalized Routine: Establish a consistent daily routine that includes dedicated times for learning, breaks, meals, and physical activity. Predictability can help your child transition between tasks more smoothly.

Task Breakdown: Break down assignments into smaller, manageable tasks. Use timers or apps to help your child work for short periods followed by breaks.

Interactive Learning: Incorporate interactive learning methods such as hands-on activities, educational games, and technology that caters to their interests.

Positive Reinforcement: Implement a reward system for completing tasks or staying focused. Positive reinforcement can motivate your child to stay engaged and on track.

Multi-Sensory Approach: Engage multiple senses during learning. Incorporate touch, movement, and visuals to enhance engagement and retention.

Movement Breaks: Allow for short movement breaks to help release excess energy and improve focus. Quick stretches, jumping jacks, or a short walk can be beneficial.

Nutrition and Hydration: Provide balanced meals and snacks that support brain function. Avoid excessive sugar and consider foods rich in protein, whole grains, and healthy fats.

Regular Exercise: Physical activity helps reduce restlessness and can improve attention span. Incorporate regular exercise into your child's routine.

Parental Support: Offer guidance and supervision without being overly controlling. Help them stay organized, set goals, and monitor their progress.

Technology Use: Use technology wisely. Educational apps and tools can enhance learning, but set limits to prevent overstimulation.

Communication: Maintain open communication with your child's teachers and therapists. Regularly discuss their progress, challenges, and strategies that work best.

Mindfulness and Relaxation: Teach relaxation techniques like deep breathing, meditation, or mindfulness exercises to help your child manage anxiety and improve focus.

Social Interaction: Provide opportunities for social interaction with peers, whether through virtual playdates or small gatherings. Social engagement contributes to emotional well-being.

Sleep Schedule: Establish a consistent sleep schedule to ensure your child gets adequate rest. Sleep is crucial for maintaining attention and cognitive function.

Patience and Flexibility: Understand that progress might be gradual. Be patient and adaptable, adjusting your strategies based on your child's feedback and needs.

Remember that each child with ADHD is unique, so it's important to tailor your approach to their individual preferences and strengths. Regularly reassess the learning environment and make necessary adjustments to continue supporting their growth and development.

6.2 Effective Study Techniques for Children with ADHD

Here are some effective study techniques for children with ADHD:

Structured Environment: Create a clutter-free and organized study area. Minimize distractions by removing unnecessary items and ensuring good lighting.

Consistent Routine: Establish a regular study routine with specific times for studying, breaks, and leisure activities. Consistency helps children with ADHD manage their time and expectations better.

Chunking Information: Break down study materials into smaller, manageable chunks. This prevents overwhelming feelings and makes it easier for children to focus on one piece of information at a time.

Use of Visual Aids: Visual aids like charts, graphs, and color-coding can help organize information and make it more engaging for visual learners. They can also aid in memory retention.

Multisensory Learning: Incorporate multiple senses into studying. Encourage hands-on activities, such as using manipulatives or drawing diagrams, to help reinforce learning.

Active Learning Strategies: Encourage participation through interactive techniques like discussions, role-playing, or teaching the material to someone else. Active engagement can improve focus and retention.

Short Study Sessions: ADHD children might find it challenging to sustain attention for extended periods.

Break study sessions into shorter intervals (e.g., 20-30 minutes) with breaks in between.

Frequent Breaks: Allow regular breaks during study sessions. These breaks can provide an opportunity for movement, relaxation, and resetting focus.

Incorporate Movement: Integrating movement into study breaks can help release excess energy and enhance concentration. Activities like stretching, jumping jacks, or a short walk can be effective.

Goal Setting: Set clear goals for each study session. This provides a sense of accomplishment and direction, which can help maintain motivation.

Mindfulness Techniques: Teach relaxation and mindfulness techniques like deep breathing or meditation to help manage stress and improve focus.

Use of Timers: Timers can be helpful for creating a sense of urgency during study sessions. Set a timer for work intervals and breaks to maintain a productive rhythm.

Variety in Materials: Use a mix of study materials, such as videos, podcasts, and interactive online resources, to keep learning engaging and prevent monotony.

Positive Reinforcement: Offer rewards or positive reinforcement for completing study tasks. This can boost motivation and make the studying experience more enjoyable.

Self-Regulation Strategies: Teach children to recognize when their focus is waning and provide them with strategies to self-regulate, such as taking a short break or switching tasks.

Utilize Interests: Incorporate the child's interests into the study material whenever possible. This can make learning more relevant and engaging.

Parental and Teacher Support: Maintain open communication between parents, teachers, and any special education professionals involved. Collaboration ensures that strategies are consistent across different environments.

Remember that every child is unique, so it's important to observe and adapt these techniques to suit the individual needs and preferences of the child with ADHD. Regularly assessing their progress and adjusting the strategies accordingly will contribute to their academic success and overall well-being.

6.3 Accommodations and Support in the Classroom for your adhd child

Supporting a child with ADHD in the classroom involves creating an environment that addresses their unique needs and helps them thrive academically, socially, and emotionally. Here are some in-depth strategies and accommodations that can be beneficial:

Individualized Education Plan (IEP) or 504 Plan: Collaborate with the school to develop an IEP or 504 plan that outlines specific accommodations and modifications tailored to your child's needs. This might include extended time for assignments and tests, preferential seating, frequent breaks, and more.

Structured Routine: Establish a consistent daily routine that includes clear schedules and transitions. Visual aids like charts or timers can help your child anticipate and understand the flow of the day.

Physical Environment: Arrange the classroom to minimize distractions. Provide a designated quiet area for focused work and consider using noise-canceling headphones when needed.

Clear Instructions: Break down tasks and instructions into smaller, manageable steps. Use visual cues and verbal reminders to help your child stay on track.

Flexible Seating: Allow options for flexible seating arrangements, such as standing desks or fidget tools, to help your child release excess energy and maintain focus.

Multisensory Learning: Incorporate a variety of sensory experiences into lessons, such as hands-on activities, movement, and interactive technology, to engage different learning styles.

Positive Reinforcement: Implement a reward system to encourage desired behaviors. Praise and rewards for staying focused, completing tasks, and following instructions can be motivating.

Small Group or One-on-One Instruction: Provide opportunities for your child to work with the teacher in a smaller group or individually for personalized attention and support.

Chunking Information: Present information in smaller chunks to prevent overwhelming your child. Use headings, bullet points, and visual aids to make content more digestible.

Regular Communication: Maintain open communication between teachers, parents, and any specialists involved in your child's education. This ensures everyone is on the same page and can make necessary adjustments as needed.

Executive Functioning Support: Teach organizational skills, time management techniques, and strategies for planning and prioritizing tasks. This can be done through explicit instruction and modeling.

Movement Breaks: Incorporate short movement breaks into the day to allow your child to release energy and refocus. These breaks can help improve attention span and reduce restlessness.

Peer Support: Encourage peer interactions and positive social relationships. Collaborative projects and group activities can help your child develop social skills and build connections with classmates.

Self-Advocacy Skills: Teach your child about ADHD and their individual needs. Empower them to communicate their needs to teachers and peers, fostering a sense of self-awareness and independence.

Emotional Regulation Strategies: Help your child develop strategies for managing emotions and frustration. Breathing exercises, mindfulness techniques, and self-calming strategies can be useful.

Remember that every child with ADHD is unique, so it's essential to continuously assess and adjust strategies based on your child's progress and needs. Regular communication with teachers and professionals can contribute to a collaborative and supportive learning environment.

6.4 Advocating for your Child's Educational Needs

Advocating for your child's educational needs is a vital aspect of ensuring they receive the support and resources necessary for their growth and development. This process involves actively working with educators, administrators, and other professionals to create an optimal learning environment tailored to your child's individual requirements. Here's a more in-depth guide on how to effectively advocate for your child's educational needs:

Understand Your Child's Needs: Begin by comprehensively understanding your child's strengths, weaknesses, learning style, and any special requirements they may have. This could involve consulting with teachers, therapists, and specialists to gain a thorough understanding of their educational profile.

Build Positive Relationships: Cultivate positive relationships with your child's teachers, school administrators, and support staff. Open and respectful communication lays the foundation for successful advocacy.

Know Your Rights: Familiarize yourself with the laws and regulations related to special education and accommodations in your region. In the United States, for instance, the Individuals with Disabilities Education Act (IDEA) provides guidelines for students with disabilities.

Gather Documentation: Collect relevant documents such as medical reports, assessment results, and any previous Individualized Education Programs (IEPs) or

504 plans. These documents provide a clear picture of your child's needs and help in advocating effectively.

Collaborate on an IEP or 504 Plan: If your child requires special accommodations, work closely with the school to create an Individualized Education Program (IEP) or a 504 plan. These documents outline the support and modifications your child needs to succeed academically and socially.

Prepare for Meetings: Before meetings with educators and administrators, outline your child's needs, goals, and the specific accommodations you believe would be beneficial. This preparation demonstrates your commitment and knowledge, making your advocacy more effective.

Be Assertive but Respectful: When discussing your child's needs, be assertive in advocating for what you believe is necessary, but maintain a respectful and cooperative tone. Collaboration yields better results than confrontation.

Request Regular Updates: Stay informed about your child's progress by requesting regular updates from teachers and support staff. This helps you gauge the effectiveness of the accommodations and make adjustments if necessary.

Problem-Solve Together: If challenges arise, work together with the school to find solutions. Approach problems as opportunities to improve your child's educational experience rather than as roadblocks.

Consider Outside Support: If you encounter difficulties in advocating for your child's needs, consider seeking advice from educational advocates, support groups, or legal experts specializing in educational rights.

Monitor and Adjust: Regularly review and adjust your child's IEP or 504 plan as needed. Children's needs evolve, and it's essential to ensure that the accommodations provided remain relevant and effective.

Celebrate Progress: Acknowledge and celebrate your child's educational achievements, both big and small. Positive reinforcement boosts their confidence and motivation.

Remember, effective advocacy is an ongoing process that requires patience, persistence, and collaboration. By actively participating in your child's education and advocating for their needs, you're helping to create an environment where they can thrive academically and personally.

Chapter 7

Fostering Social Skills: Building Positive Relationships and Peer Interactions

Fostering social skills is crucial for building positive relationships and facilitating successful peer interactions. These skills enable individuals to connect, communicate, and collaborate effectively. Here's an in-depth exploration of the topic:

Understanding Social Skills:
Social skills encompass a range of abilities that allow individuals to interact with others harmoniously. These skills include communication, empathy, active listening, conflict resolution, cooperation, and understanding non-verbal cues. Developing these skills is vital for creating meaningful connections and navigating social situations.

Importance of Positive Relationships:
Positive relationships contribute to emotional well-being and overall life satisfaction. They provide support, reduce stress, and enhance mental health. Teaching individuals to cultivate empathy, respect, and effective communication helps them establish and maintain healthy connections.

Peer Interactions in Different Settings:
Peer interactions occur in various contexts, such as school, work, and social events. These interactions play a significant role in personal and professional development. Guiding individuals on appropriate behavior, active listening, and collaborative problem-solving helps them navigate these settings successfully.

Effective Communication:
Clear and respectful communication is a cornerstone of healthy relationships. Teaching individuals to express themselves clearly, while also actively listening to others, prevents misunderstandings and promotes a positive atmosphere. Role-playing and communication exercises can enhance these skills.

Empathy and Perspective-Taking:
Empathy involves understanding and sharing the feelings of others. Encouraging individuals to see

situations from different perspectives fosters empathy, reducing conflict and enhancing mutual understanding. Discussing diverse backgrounds and experiences can help broaden one's perspective.

Conflict Resolution:
Conflicts are natural in any relationship. Teaching conflict resolution skills, such as staying calm, identifying issues, and seeking common ground, empowers individuals to address disagreements constructively. These skills prevent escalation and nurture stronger connections.

Cooperation and Teamwork:
Collaboration is essential in both personal and professional settings. Engaging in group activities, projects, or team sports nurtures cooperation and teamwork skills. Individuals learn to value others' contributions, communicate effectively within groups, and collectively work toward shared goals.

Non-verbal Communication:
Non-verbal cues, such as body language, facial expressions, and tone of voice, convey messages beyond words. Helping individuals interpret and utilize non-verbal cues improves their ability to understand emotions and intentions, enhancing their social interactions.

Practicing Active Listening:
Active listening involves giving full attention to the speaker and showing genuine interest in their words. Encouraging individuals to listen without interrupting, asking clarifying questions, and responding thoughtfully promotes meaningful conversations and deeper connections.

Social Problem-Solving:
Teaching individuals how to analyze social situations, identify potential issues, and devise effective solutions prepares them to handle real-life challenges. Role-playing scenarios and discussing different approaches build their problem-solving skills.

Creating Safe Spaces:
Fostering social skills requires creating environments where individuals feel safe to express themselves and make mistakes. Such spaces encourage open communication and enable personal growth in social interactions.

In conclusion, fostering social skills involves nurturing a range of abilities that enable positive relationships and successful peer interactions. By emphasizing effective communication, empathy, conflict resolution, and cooperation, individuals can navigate various social settings with confidence and create meaningful connections. Through consistent practice, guidance, and understanding, individuals can develop strong social skills that benefit them throughout their lives.

7.1 Understanding Social Challenges Faced by Children with ADHD

Children with ADHD (Attention-Deficit/Hyperactivity Disorder) often encounter a myriad of social challenges that stem from the core symptoms of the disorder. ADHD is characterized by difficulties in sustaining attention, hyperactivity, and impulsivity. These symptoms can significantly impact a child's ability to navigate social interactions and form meaningful relationships.

One primary social challenge faced by children with ADHD is the struggle to maintain focus during conversations or group activities. Their attention may easily wander, leading to missed cues, misunderstandings, and an inability to actively participate in discussions. This can result in peers perceiving them as disinterested, aloof, or even rude, which may lead to social isolation and lower self-esteem.

Additionally, impulsivity in children with ADHD can lead to difficulties in adhering to social norms and appropriate behavior. They might interrupt others, speak out of turn, or engage in impulsive actions without considering the consequences. Such behaviors can strain friendships and make it challenging for children with ADHD to build positive connections with peers who may find their actions disruptive or disrespectful.

Moreover, hyperactivity can contribute to difficulties in engaging in cooperative play or group activities. Children with ADHD may struggle with turn-taking, sharing, and following the rules of games. This can result in frustrations for both the child with ADHD and their peers, potentially leading to exclusion and negative perceptions.

Another aspect to consider is the potential for emotional dysregulation in children with ADHD. They may experience intense emotions and have difficulty managing them, which can affect their ability to navigate conflicts or disagreements effectively. This emotional volatility can lead to strained relationships as peers may find it challenging to predict or respond to the child's emotional outbursts.

In school settings, children with ADHD might face challenges with organization and time management. They may struggle to complete assignments, forget deadlines, or lose track of materials. These difficulties can hinder their academic performance and contribute to feelings of inadequacy, making it harder to relate to their classmates.

Support from parents, teachers, and mental health professionals is crucial in helping children with ADHD overcome these social challenges. Teaching them social skills, self-regulation techniques, and providing a structured environment can significantly improve their ability to navigate social interactions and form meaningful connections. It's important to recognize that while ADHD presents unique social difficulties, with the right interventions and understanding, children with ADHD can thrive socially and emotionally.

7.2 Teaching Social Skills and Problem-solving Strategies

Teaching social skills and problem-solving strategies is crucial for individuals to navigate various interpersonal situations and challenges successfully. Whether in personal relationships, work environments, or other social settings, these skills play a vital role in effective communication, conflict resolution, and collaboration.

1. Importance of Teaching Social Skills and Problem-solving:

Social skills encompass a range of abilities, including active listening, empathy, communication, and assertiveness. These skills facilitate healthy interactions and help avoid misunderstandings.
Problem-solving strategies involve critical thinking, analysis, and creativity to find solutions to various challenges. Teaching these strategies equips individuals with the tools to tackle both simple and complex issues.
2. Structured Curriculum:

Develop a structured curriculum that progressively introduces and reinforces social skills and problem-solving techniques. Begin with foundational skills and gradually move to more advanced concepts. Incorporate real-life scenarios to provide practical examples for learners. This enables them to apply the skills in context.

3. Active Learning:

Utilize interactive methods such as role-playing, group discussions, and case studies to engage learners. These techniques encourage active participation and practical application of skills.

4. Communication Skills:

Focus on effective verbal and nonverbal communication. Teach active listening, clear expression of thoughts, and understanding body language cues.

Address the importance of adapting communication style to different situations and audiences.

5. Empathy and Perspective-taking:

Help learners develop empathy by encouraging them to understand and consider the feelings and perspectives of others.

Role-playing exercises can be particularly effective in enhancing empathy, as they require participants to step into another person's shoes.

6. Conflict Resolution:

Teach conflict resolution techniques, emphasizing negotiation, compromise, and finding win-win solutions.
Use case studies to illustrate common conflicts and guide learners through the process of resolving them constructively.

7. Decision-making and Critical Thinking:

Train individuals in effective decision-making by teaching them to analyze situations, weigh pros and cons, and consider potential consequences.
Encourage critical thinking by presenting open-ended problems that require thoughtful evaluation and innovative solutions.

8. Stress Management and Resilience:

Acknowledge the importance of managing stress and handling setbacks. Teach strategies like mindfulness, deep breathing, and positive reframing.
Help learners build resilience, enabling them to bounce back from challenges and setbacks with a positive mindset.

9. Cultural Sensitivity:

Highlight the significance of understanding and respecting cultural differences. This fosters inclusivity and helps avoid misunderstandings.

Provide examples that showcase how cultural norms and values can impact communication and interactions.

10. Continuous Assessment and Feedback:

Regularly assess learners' progress through quizzes, role-playing assessments, and group activities.

Provide constructive feedback to help individuals understand their strengths and areas for improvement.

Incorporating these aspects into a comprehensive teaching approach can effectively equip individuals with the social skills and problem-solving strategies necessary for successful interactions and navigating diverse environments. Remember, the ultimate goal is to empower learners to handle a wide range of interpersonal situations with confidence and effectiveness.

7.3 Encouraging Healthy Peer Relationships and Friendships for your adhd child

Encouraging healthy peer relationships and friendships for a child with ADHD involves creating a supportive environment, fostering social skills development, and maintaining effective communication. Here's an in-depth guide to help you navigate this process:

Understanding ADHD: Educate yourself, your child, and their friends about ADHD. Knowledge about the condition reduces stigma, improves empathy, and enhances acceptance.

Structured Social Opportunities: Engage your child in structured activities that cater to their interests. Sports, art classes, clubs, or hobby groups provide common ground for forming friendships.

Social Skills Training: Work with a therapist or counselor experienced in ADHD to develop social skills. Role-playing, teaching conversation etiquette, and practicing effective communication techniques can boost your child's confidence.

Mediation and Conflict Resolution: Teach your child how to manage disagreements and conflicts in a healthy manner. Role-model effective conflict resolution strategies to help them navigate challenges.

Playdates: Organize playdates in a controlled and comfortable environment. Smaller gatherings allow your child to develop connections in a less overwhelming setting.

Setting Realistic Expectations: Understand that your child's friendships might differ from typical relationships. Encourage them to make friends who appreciate their uniqueness and strengths.

Friendship Coaching: Provide guidance on reading social cues, taking turns, and interpreting nonverbal communication. Offer subtle prompts to help your child navigate social interactions.

Building Self-Esteem: Encourage your child's interests and celebrate their achievements. A strong sense of self-worth contributes to positive peer interactions.

Inclusive Social Groups: Seek out inclusive activities or groups where your child can meet others who share similar challenges. This can help them feel less isolated and more understood.

Parental Involvement: Communicate with other parents to foster understanding. Share your child's needs and preferences to create an inclusive environment.

Involve Teachers: Collaborate with teachers to create opportunities for positive social interactions at school. They can facilitate group projects, peer mentoring, or cooperative learning activities.

Online Friendships: Monitor your child's online interactions and guide them on safe and appropriate online behavior. Virtual friendships can provide additional social outlets.

Empathy and Perspective-Taking: Teach your child about empathy and understanding others' feelings. Role-playing scenarios can help them develop these skills.

Consistent Routine: Maintaining a consistent routine can help your child manage their ADHD symptoms, leading to better interactions with peers.

Praise and Encouragement: Acknowledge your child's efforts in making friends and maintaining relationships. Positive reinforcement boosts their motivation to engage with peers.

Open Communication: Keep the lines of communication open. Regularly check in with your child about their social experiences, challenges, and triumphs.

Social Scripts: Provide your child with simple scripts for initiating conversations or joining group activities. This can ease their social anxiety.

Resilience Building: Help your child develop resilience in the face of setbacks or friendship challenges. Discuss strategies for coping with disappointments.

Remember that building friendships is a gradual process, and every child is unique. Tailor your approach based on your child's personality, interests, and comfort level. Be patient and supportive, and celebrate every step forward in their social journey.

7.4 Addressing Bullying and Stigma for your adhd child

Addressing bullying and stigma for a child with ADHD requires a multifaceted approach that involves communication, education, empowerment, and support from various stakeholders, including parents, teachers, peers, and the child themselves. Here's an in-depth look at strategies to effectively tackle this issue:

Parental Involvement and Communication:

Maintain open communication with your child about their experiences at school. Encourage them to share any incidents of bullying or stigmatization they may have encountered.
Provide a safe and non-judgmental space for your child to express their feelings and concerns.
Build a strong relationship with your child's teachers and school staff. Regularly discuss your child's ADHD and any challenges they may face.
Educating Peers and Teachers:

Organize awareness programs in the school to educate students, teachers, and staff about ADHD. This can help reduce stigma by promoting understanding.
Provide information on the neurological basis of ADHD, highlighting that it's not a result of laziness or lack of discipline.
Empowerment and Self-Esteem:

Help your child build self-confidence by focusing on their strengths and achievements.

Encourage them to pursue hobbies and interests that they excel in, boosting their self-esteem.
Social Skills Training:

Collaborate with therapists or counselors to provide your child with social skills training. This can help them navigate social interactions more effectively and respond to bullying with assertiveness.
Anti-Bullying Programs:

Advocate for the implementation of anti-bullying programs in your child's school. These programs can promote a culture of respect and tolerance.
Individualized Education Plan (IEP):

Work with the school to develop an IEP tailored to your child's needs. This plan can include accommodations and strategies to address their ADHD-related challenges.
Building Resilience:

Teach your child strategies to cope with stress and adversity. This can involve mindfulness techniques, deep breathing exercises, and positive self-talk.
Promoting Peer Support:

Encourage your child to build friendships with peers who are understanding and supportive. Peer support can help counteract the negative effects of bullying.
Counseling and Therapy:

If your child is experiencing emotional distress due to bullying, consider seeking professional counseling or therapy. A trained therapist can help them process their feelings and develop coping mechanisms.
Legal Protection:

Familiarize yourself with the laws and policies related to bullying and disability rights in your region. If necessary, take appropriate action to protect your child's rights.
Advocacy:

Advocate for ADHD awareness and acceptance within the community. Join local support groups or online forums to connect with other parents facing similar challenges.
Remember that addressing bullying and stigma for a child with ADHD is an ongoing process that requires collaboration and persistence. By implementing these strategies, you can create a supportive environment that nurtures your child's well-being and helps them thrive despite challenges.

Chapter 8

Supporting Healthy Lifestyle Habits: Nutrition, Sleep, and Exercise

Promoting healthy lifestyle habits for a child with ADHD involves a comprehensive approach that encompasses nutrition, sleep, and exercise. Here's an in-depth overview of each aspect:

Nutrition:

Balanced Diet: Provide a well-rounded diet rich in whole grains, lean proteins, healthy fats, and a variety of fruits and vegetables.

Omega-3 Fatty Acids: Foods like fatty fish (salmon, mackerel) and flaxseeds containing omega-3s have been linked to improved cognitive function and focus in ADHD.

Protein-Rich Foods: Incorporate lean protein sources such as poultry, beans, nuts, and yogurt. Proteins aid in neurotransmitter production, supporting attention and mood regulation.

Limit Sugar and Processed Foods: Reduce consumption of sugary snacks, sodas, and highly processed foods. These can lead to energy crashes and worsen ADHD symptoms.

Consistent Meals: Ensure regular, balanced meals and snacks to prevent fluctuations in blood sugar levels, which can impact attention and mood.

Sleep:

Consistent Sleep Schedule: Establish a consistent sleep routine with a fixed bedtime and wake-up time, even on weekends.

Bedroom Environment: Create a calming sleep environment with dim lighting, comfortable bedding, and a noise-free atmosphere.

Screen Time Reduction: Limit screen time (TV, tablets, smartphones) before bedtime, as blue light can interfere with the production of melatonin, a sleep-regulating hormone.

Relaxation Techniques: Encourage relaxation activities before bed, such as reading, gentle stretching, or deep breathing exercises, to help transition into sleep.

Physical Activity: Ensure your child gets enough physical activity during the day to help promote better sleep at night.

Exercise:

Regular Physical Activity: Engage your child in regular exercise to release endorphins, improve focus, and regulate energy levels.

Varied Activities: Encourage a mix of activities they enjoy, such as sports, swimming, biking, or even yoga, to keep them engaged.

Outdoor Play: Time spent outdoors exposes them to natural light and fresh air, both of which can positively impact mood and attention.

Structured Routine: Incorporate physical activities into their daily routine, ensuring a consistent schedule that supports their overall well-being.

Social Interaction: Participating in group activities or team sports can help your child develop social skills and build self-esteem.

Remember, each child is unique, so it's essential to work closely with healthcare professionals and possibly a registered dietitian or nutritionist. These experts can tailor recommendations to your child's specific needs, taking into account any allergies, sensitivities, or preferences. Additionally, involving your child in the decision-making process and making these lifestyle changes as a family effort can increase their motivation and success in adopting these healthy habits.

8.1 The Impact of Nutrition on ADHD Symptoms

Attention Deficit Hyperactivity Disorder (ADHD) is a neurodevelopmental disorder characterized by symptoms of inattention, hyperactivity, and impulsivity. While genetics and neurological factors play a significant role in the development of ADHD, there is growing interest in understanding the potential impact of nutrition on the severity of its symptoms.

Nutritional Factors and ADHD:
Several nutritional factors have been studied for their potential impact on ADHD symptoms:

Omega-3 Fatty Acids: Omega-3 fatty acids, particularly EPA (eicosapentaenoic acid) and DHA (docosahexaenoic acid), are essential for brain health. Some studies suggest that individuals with ADHD might have lower levels of omega-3 fatty acids in their blood, which could affect neural functioning. Supplementation with omega-3 fatty acids has shown mixed results in improving ADHD symptoms, with some studies reporting modest benefits in reducing hyperactivity and impulsivity.

Micronutrients: Deficiencies in certain micronutrients, such as iron, zinc, magnesium, and vitamin D, have been associated with ADHD symptoms. Iron is crucial for neurotransmitter production, while zinc and magnesium play roles in neural transmission and regulation. Vitamin D has been linked to brain development and function. However, while some studies suggest that addressing these deficiencies could alleviate ADHD symptoms, more research is needed to establish definitive links.

Food Additives and Sugar: Some studies have explored the impact of food additives, artificial colors, and high sugar intake on ADHD symptoms. While there's anecdotal evidence that certain food additives might exacerbate hyperactivity in susceptible individuals, the overall consensus is inconclusive. High sugar intake, on the other hand, is not consistently linked to worsening ADHD symptoms, but maintaining a balanced diet is generally recommended.

Protein and Carbohydrates: The balance between protein and carbohydrate intake can influence neurotransmitter production and regulation. Protein-rich foods provide the building blocks for neurotransmitters like dopamine and norepinephrine, which are associated with attention and focus. Complex carbohydrates can help stabilize blood sugar levels, potentially reducing fluctuations in energy and concentration.

Dietary Strategies:
It's important to note that while some studies suggest a relationship between nutrition and ADHD symptoms, individual responses can vary significantly. Dietary strategies that might be considered include:

Balanced Diet: Focus on a balanced diet rich in whole grains, lean proteins, healthy fats, and a variety of fruits and vegetables.

Omega-3 Supplementation: Incorporate sources of omega-3 fatty acids, such as fatty fish (salmon, mackerel), flaxseeds, and walnuts. Consult a healthcare professional before considering supplements.

Micronutrient-Rich Foods: Include foods that are good sources of iron, zinc, magnesium, and vitamin D, such as lean meats, nuts, seeds, dairy products, and fortified cereals.

Limit Processed Foods: Minimize consumption of heavily processed foods high in additives, preservatives, and artificial colors.

Conclusion:

The relationship between nutrition and ADHD symptoms is complex and not fully understood. While some nutritional factors might influence symptom severity, there is no one-size-fits-all dietary approach. Individuals with ADHD should focus on maintaining a balanced diet and consult healthcare professionals before making significant dietary changes or considering supplementation. Further research is needed to establish definitive links between nutrition and ADHD symptoms.

8.2 Establishing Healthy Sleep Patterns and Routines for your adhd child

Establishing healthy sleep patterns and routines for a child with ADHD is crucial for their overall well-being and daily functioning. ADHD, or Attention Deficit Hyperactivity Disorder, often presents challenges in regulating sleep due to difficulties in attention, impulse control, and hyperactivity. Creating a structured sleep routine can greatly improve their sleep quality, which in turn positively impacts their ADHD symptoms and daily functioning.

Consistent Sleep Schedule: Set a consistent sleep schedule for your child, including weekends. Regular bedtimes and wake-up times help regulate their internal body clock and improve the quality of sleep. This consistency reinforces their natural sleep-wake cycle, making it easier for them to fall asleep and wake up refreshed.

Bedtime Routine: Establish a calming bedtime routine that signals the transition from wakefulness to sleep. This routine might include activities like reading a book, taking a warm bath, or practicing relaxation techniques. Engaging in calming activities helps lower arousal levels and prepares the mind and body for sleep.

Limit Screen Time: The blue light emitted by screens can interfere with the production of melatonin, a hormone that regulates sleep. Limit screen time at least an hour before bedtime. Encourage activities that do not involve screens, such as reading a physical book or engaging in creative play.

Create a Sleep-Inducing Environment: Design the bedroom to promote sleep. Keep the room dark, quiet, and at a comfortable temperature. Consider using blackout curtains, white noise machines, or soft lighting to create a calming atmosphere conducive to sleep.

Physical Activity: Regular physical activity during the day can help tire out an energetic child and promote better sleep at night. However, avoid intense physical activity close to bedtime, as it might have the opposite effect.

Diet and Nutrition: Pay attention to your child's diet, particularly in the hours leading up to bedtime. Avoid large meals, caffeine, and sugary snacks close to bedtime, as they can disrupt sleep. Instead, opt for light, healthy snacks if necessary.

Limit Stimulants: Medications used to manage ADHD symptoms, such as stimulants, can affect sleep. Consult your child's healthcare provider about the timing of medication doses to minimize their impact on sleep.

Engage in Daylight Exposure: Natural light exposure during the day helps regulate the sleep-wake cycle. Encourage outdoor activities and sunlight exposure, especially in the morning.

Limit Naps: While short naps can be beneficial, excessive daytime napping can interfere with nighttime sleep. If your child naps during the day, ensure that the nap is relatively short and not too close to bedtime.

Bedroom as a Sleep Space: It's important to establish the bedroom as a dedicated sleep space. Encourage your child to associate the bedroom with restful sleep by avoiding activities like studying or playing in bed.

Consistent Wake-Up Time: Just as having a consistent bedtime is important, having a consistent wake-up time helps regulate the body's internal clock. This consistency reinforces the sleep schedule and improves overall sleep quality.

Patience and Flexibility: Adjusting to a new sleep routine can take time, especially for children with ADHD. Be patient and understanding as you work together to establish healthy sleep patterns. If changes need to be made, do so gradually.

Remember that each child is unique, and what works for one may not work for another. It's important to tailor the sleep routine to your child's specific needs and preferences. Consulting a pediatrician or a sleep specialist can provide valuable insights and guidance in developing a sleep plan that effectively supports your child's ADHD management and overall well-being.

8.3 The Benefits of Physical Activity for Children with ADHD

Physical activity can have profound benefits for children with Attention Deficit Hyperactivity Disorder (ADHD), extending beyond just promoting physical health. Research has shown that engaging in regular physical activity can positively impact various aspects of their lives, including cognitive function, behavior, emotional well-being, and overall quality of life.

Improved Executive Function: Children with ADHD often struggle with executive functions like attention control, working memory, and impulse control. Physical activity, particularly aerobic exercises, has been found to enhance these cognitive functions. Regular physical activity can improve focus, decision-making, and planning skills, which are crucial for academic and everyday tasks.

Enhanced Brain Structure: Physical activity triggers the release of neurotransmitters such as dopamine and norepinephrine, which play a crucial role in regulating attention and mood. Additionally, exercise stimulates the growth of new neurons and improves brain connectivity, leading to enhanced cognitive abilities and reduced ADHD symptoms.

Reduced Hyperactivity and Impulsivity: Physical activity provides an outlet for excess energy and restlessness often seen in children with ADHD. Engaging in sports, running, or other active games can help channel and manage hyperactivity, leading to better self-regulation and reduced impulsivity.

Emotional Regulation: Children with ADHD might struggle with emotional regulation and mood swings. Physical activity triggers the release of endorphins, which are natural mood enhancers. Regular exercise can help stabilize mood, decrease anxiety and depression, and improve overall emotional well-being.

Social Skills Development: Participating in group sports or physical activities can provide children with ADHD opportunities to develop social skills. Team-based activities teach cooperation, communication, and problem-solving, which can contribute to improved interpersonal relationships and self-confidence.

Increased Self-Esteem: Success in physical activities, even small achievements, can boost self-esteem in children with ADHD. As they master new skills or improve their performance, they gain a sense of accomplishment that extends beyond the physical realm.

Better Sleep Patterns: Many children with ADHD experience sleep difficulties. Engaging in regular physical activity can help regulate sleep patterns, leading to improved quality and duration of sleep. Better sleep, in turn, contributes to enhanced focus and cognitive function during waking hours.

Alternative to Medication: While medication can be effective in managing ADHD symptoms, some parents prefer to explore non-pharmacological interventions. Physical activity can serve as an alternative or complementary strategy to medication, providing benefits without potential side effects.

Long-Term Health Benefits: Encouraging physical activity in childhood establishes healthy habits that can extend into adulthood. Regular exercise reduces the risk of obesity, diabetes, cardiovascular diseases, and other health issues often associated with ADHD.

Improved Academic Performance: The cognitive benefits of physical activity can translate into better academic performance. Enhanced focus, attention, and memory can lead to improved learning outcomes and academic success for children with ADHD.

Incorporating physical activity into the daily routine of children with ADHD can be immensely beneficial. However, it's important to tailor activities to their individual preferences and needs. Consulting with healthcare professionals, educators, and specialists can help create a well-rounded approach to managing ADHD symptoms through physical activity.

8.4   Integrating   Mindfulness   and   Relaxation Techniques to your adhd child

Integrating mindfulness and relaxation techniques into the routine of a child with ADHD can have a positive impact on their emotional well-being, focus, and overall behavior. However, it's important to note that these techniques are not standalone treatments but rather complementary strategies that can be used alongside other interventions.

Understanding ADHD and Mindfulness: ADHD is a neurodevelopmental disorder characterized by difficulties in attention, impulse control, and hyperactivity. Mindfulness involves cultivating awareness of the present moment without judgment. It can help children with ADHD become more aware of their thoughts, feelings, and bodily sensations, allowing them to better regulate their reactions.

Mindful Breathing: Teach your child to focus on their breath. Inhaling and exhaling deeply can help them stay centered and calm. Encourage them to notice the sensation of their breath as it moves in and out of their body.

Body Scan: Guide your child through a body scan exercise. This involves systematically focusing their attention on different parts of their body, promoting relaxation and awareness. This practice can help them become attuned to their physical sensations and reduce tension.

Mindful Observation: Engage your child in mindful observation of their surroundings. Encourage them to notice details they might not have noticed before, like colors, textures, and sounds. This exercise can enhance their ability to sustain attention and appreciate the present moment.

Mindful Movement: Incorporate mindful movement activities like yoga or tai chi. These practices combine physical movement with breath awareness, helping your child develop better body awareness and self-regulation skills.

Guided Imagery: Use guided imagery exercises to help your child create mental images that promote relaxation and focus. These images can be calming scenes, like a peaceful beach or a quiet forest, and can help them reduce stress and anxiety.

Progressive Muscle Relaxation: Teach your child how to systematically tense and relax different muscle groups. This technique can alleviate physical tension and promote a sense of relaxation.

Mindful Eating: Encourage your child to eat mindfully, paying close attention to the taste, texture, and smell of their food. This can help them develop better eating habits and regulate their impulses.

Consistency is Key: Integrate these techniques into your child's daily routine consistently. Short sessions, around 5-10 minutes, can be more effective than longer sessions, especially for children with shorter attention spans.

Model Mindfulness: Children learn by example, so practice mindfulness yourself. When your child sees you engaging in these techniques, they're more likely to adopt them.

Patience and Flexibility: Remember that every child is different. Be patient and flexible in your approach, and adjust the techniques based on your child's preferences and needs.

Professional Guidance: While mindfulness and relaxation techniques can be beneficial, they should not replace professional medical or psychological interventions. Consult with a healthcare provider or therapist to develop a comprehensive plan for managing your child's ADHD.

By integrating these techniques into your child's routine, you can help them develop self-awareness, emotional regulation, and attention skills that can positively impact their overall well-being and ability to manage their ADHD symptoms.

Chapter 9

Collaborating with Professionals: Working with Therapists, Doctors, and Specialists

Collaborating with professionals when supporting a child with ADHD involves a multi-faceted approach that requires coordination, communication, and a deep understanding of the child's needs. Here's an in-depth look at how to effectively work with therapists, doctors, and specialists for your child with ADHD:

Clear Diagnosis and Assessment: Begin by obtaining a comprehensive diagnosis from a qualified medical professional, such as a pediatrician or child psychiatrist. A thorough assessment should involve gathering information from parents, teachers, and the child's own observations to accurately diagnose ADHD and any potential coexisting conditions.

Building a Team: Create a team of professionals that may include a child psychiatrist, pediatrician, clinical psychologist, educational psychologist, occupational therapist, speech-language pathologist, and special education teacher, among others. This interdisciplinary approach ensures comprehensive support.

Open Communication: Regularly communicate with each professional involved in your child's care. Share updates on progress, challenges, and any changes in medication or treatment. This collaboration helps ensure everyone is on the same page and adjustments can be made as needed.

Setting Clear Goals: Work together with the professionals to set clear and achievable goals for your child's development and well-being. These goals should be specific, measurable, attainable, relevant, and time-bound (SMART).

Individualized Treatment Plan: Each child with ADHD is unique, and their treatment plan should reflect their individual needs. Collaborate with specialists to develop an individualized plan that may include behavioral therapy, medication, educational accommodations, and lifestyle modifications.

Behavioral Interventions: Behavioral therapies, such as Cognitive Behavioral Therapy (CBT) and Parent Management Training (PMT), can help children develop coping strategies, improve self-regulation, and manage impulsivity and hyperactivity.

Medication Management: If medication is part of the treatment plan, work closely with a child psychiatrist to monitor its effects and adjust dosages if necessary. Regular check-ins are crucial to ensure the medication is effective and well-tolerated.

Educational Support: Collaborate with teachers, special education professionals, and school counselors to create an Individualized Education Plan (IEP) or a 504 Plan. These documents outline specific accommodations and support your child needs to succeed academically.

Therapeutic Support: If your child requires therapy beyond behavioral interventions, consider involving a therapist or counselor who specializes in working with children with ADHD. They can provide emotional support, teach social skills, and address any related challenges.

Parental Involvement: Parents play a central role in their child's treatment. Attend therapy sessions, workshops, and training sessions to learn effective strategies for managing ADHD-related behaviors at home.

Consistency and Patience: Consistency is key in managing ADHD. Collaborate with professionals to establish consistent routines and strategies both at home and school. Be patient; progress may take time, and adjustments might be needed along the way.

Advocating for Your Child: Be an advocate for your child's needs. If you encounter challenges in accessing appropriate services or accommodations, work with professionals to navigate the system and ensure your child's rights are upheld.

Holistic Approach: Remember that treating ADHD involves addressing not only the medical and educational aspects, but also the social, emotional, and psychological well-being of your child. A holistic approach ensures a more well-rounded support system.

In summary, collaborating with professionals for your child with ADHD involves a comprehensive and collaborative approach that focuses on individualized care, open communication, and a commitment to your child's well-being. By working together with a team of experts, you can provide the best possible support for your child's development and success.

9.1 The Role of Pediatricians and Psychiatrists in ADHD Management

ADHD (Attention-Deficit/Hyperactivity Disorder) is a neurodevelopmental disorder that affects children, often continuing into adulthood. The management of ADHD typically involves a multidisciplinary approach, with pediatricians and psychiatrists playing crucial roles in different aspects of care.

Pediatricians are usually the first point of contact for parents or caregivers concerned about a child's behavior or attention difficulties. They play a fundamental role in the initial assessment and diagnosis of ADHD. Pediatricians gather information through interviews with the child's parents, teachers, and sometimes the child themselves. They use standardized assessment tools to evaluate the child's symptoms, behavior, and functioning in various settings. This comprehensive assessment helps in distinguishing ADHD from other conditions that may mimic its symptoms.

Once a diagnosis is established, pediatricians often collaborate with other professionals, such as educational psychologists, to develop a comprehensive treatment plan. This plan may include behavioral interventions, parental training, and school accommodations tailored to the child's needs. Pediatricians also closely monitor the child's growth, development, and overall well-being, ensuring that any prescribed medications are well-tolerated and effective.

On the other hand, psychiatrists bring specialized expertise in understanding the underlying neurobiology of ADHD and can provide more targeted interventions. They are often involved when the child's symptoms are severe, complicated, or when comorbid mental health issues are present. Psychiatrists can provide in-depth assessments, including neuropsychological testing, to better understand the cognitive profile of the child. This can help tailor interventions to address specific cognitive challenges.

Psychiatrists are authorized to prescribe medications for ADHD, such as stimulants and non-stimulants. These medications can help improve attention, impulse control, and hyperactivity. However, prescribing these medications requires careful consideration, as they come with potential side effects and must be closely monitored.

Collaboration between pediatricians and psychiatrists is essential for successful ADHD management. Regular communication ensures that treatment approaches are coordinated and aligned with the child's changing needs. The pediatrician may manage the overall care plan, while the psychiatrist focuses on medication management and providing additional insights into the child's cognitive functioning and emotional well-being.

In more complex cases, where behavioral interventions and medication alone might not be sufficient, a team-based approach involving pediatricians, psychiatrists, psychologists, occupational therapists, and educational specialists can offer comprehensive support. This interdisciplinary collaboration addresses the various facets of ADHD and ensures that the child's needs are holistically met.

In conclusion, the roles of pediatricians and psychiatrists in ADHD management are complementary and vital. Pediatricians are typically the front line in diagnosis, general care, and behavioral interventions, while psychiatrists bring specialized knowledge in medication management and addressing complex cases. Together, they contribute to a comprehensive and tailored approach to support children with ADHD in reaching their full potential.

9.2 Therapeutic Approaches for ADHD, including Behavioral Therapy and Medication

An in-depth overview of therapeutic approaches for ADHD, including behavioral therapy and medication.

1. Behavioral Therapy:
Behavioral therapy is a fundamental approach in managing ADHD. It focuses on teaching individuals coping strategies, organizational skills, and behavioral modifications. Some key techniques within behavioral therapy include:

Parent Training: Parents learn strategies to manage their child's behavior, set appropriate boundaries, and implement consistent routines.

Behavioral Interventions: Techniques such as token economies (reward systems), time-outs, and positive reinforcement are used to encourage desired behaviors and discourage impulsive actions.

Cognitive Behavioral Therapy (CBT): CBT helps individuals recognize and change negative thought patterns and impulsive behaviors. It's particularly effective for older children, adolescents, and adults.

Social Skills Training: This helps individuals develop interpersonal skills, such as effective communication and problem-solving, to enhance relationships and reduce social challenges.

2. Medication:
Medication is often used in conjunction with behavioral therapy to manage ADHD symptoms. Commonly prescribed medications include:

Stimulants: These are the most common medications for ADHD and include methylphenidate (e.g., Ritalin) and amphetamine-based medications (e.g., Adderall). They work by increasing the levels of certain neurotransmitters in the brain, improving focus and impulse control.

Non-Stimulants: For those who don't respond well to stimulants or have specific contraindications, non-stimulant medications like atomoxetine (Strattera) and guanfacine (Intuniv) are considered.

Combination Therapy: In some cases, a combination of medications may be prescribed to target different aspects of ADHD symptoms.

3. Other Approaches:
Apart from behavioral therapy and medication, several other approaches can be considered:

Mindfulness and Meditation: Techniques like mindfulness and meditation can help individuals with ADHD improve their attention, self-regulation, and overall well-being.

Diet and Lifestyle Changes: Some individuals find that certain dietary modifications (like reducing sugar or caffeine intake) and maintaining a healthy lifestyle (adequate sleep and regular exercise) can positively impact their ADHD symptoms.

Educational Support: Individuals with ADHD may benefit from educational accommodations, such as extended time for assignments or exams, to help them succeed academically.

Support Groups and Counseling: Engaging in support groups or counseling can provide emotional support, coping strategies, and a sense of community for individuals and their families.

It's important to note that the most effective treatment plan often involves a combination of approaches tailored to the individual's needs. Consulting with healthcare professionals, such as psychiatrists, psychologists, or pediatricians, is crucial in determining the best course of action for managing ADHD symptoms.

9.3 Seeking Additional Support from Occupational Therapists, Speech Therapists for your adhd child

Seeking additional support from occupational therapists and speech therapists for your child with ADHD can be a beneficial step in their overall development and well-being. ADHD, or Attention Deficit Hyperactivity Disorder, is a neurodevelopmental condition that can impact a child's ability to focus, regulate impulses, and control their behavior. While medication and behavioral interventions are often part of the treatment plan, therapeutic support from occupational and speech therapists can play a pivotal role in addressing specific challenges associated with ADHD.

Occupational therapy focuses on enhancing a child's ability to engage in everyday activities and tasks. Children with ADHD may struggle with motor skills, organization, sensory processing, and self-regulation. An occupational therapist can assess your child's specific needs and design interventions to improve these areas. For example, they might work on fine and gross motor skills to enhance handwriting and coordination, teach organizational strategies to manage tasks, or develop sensory integration techniques to help with focus and self-calming.

Speech therapy, on the other hand, can aid children with ADHD who experience difficulties in communication and language skills. Some children with ADHD may struggle with expressive and receptive language, social communication, and pragmatic language use. A speech therapist can conduct assessments to identify language deficits and tailor interventions to improve communication abilities. This might involve enhancing vocabulary, teaching effective communication strategies, and addressing challenges in social interactions.

Collaboration between occupational and speech therapists can be particularly beneficial for children with ADHD, as their challenges often overlap. Occupational therapy can address motor and sensory difficulties that might impact speech and language development, while speech therapy can focus on improving communication skills that are essential for effective social interactions.

When seeking support from these therapists, it's important to find professionals with experience working with children with ADHD. A multidisciplinary approach involving parents, educators, therapists, and medical professionals can create a comprehensive support system tailored to the child's needs. Regular communication between therapists and the child's support network ensures a coordinated effort and allows for adjustments to the treatment plan as progress is made.

In conclusion, seeking additional support from occupational therapists and speech therapists for your child with ADHD can provide them with targeted interventions to address specific challenges related to motor skills, sensory processing, organization, and communication. This holistic approach can contribute significantly to your child's overall development and quality of life.

9.4 Building a Strong Support Network for adhd Parents

Building a strong support network for parents of children with ADHD is crucial to navigate the challenges and complexities that come with the condition. Here's an in-depth guide on how to create such a network:

Education and Awareness:
Begin by educating yourself about ADHD. Understand the symptoms, treatment options, and strategies to manage it. This knowledge will empower you to make informed decisions and advocate for your child effectively.

Connect with Professionals:
Seek guidance from healthcare professionals, such as pediatricians, psychologists, or child psychiatrists. They can provide accurate diagnoses, recommend suitable treatment plans, and connect you with local resources.

Join Support Groups:
Participating in support groups, whether in-person or online, can offer a sense of belonging and

understanding. Connecting with other parents who are going through similar experiences can provide emotional relief and practical advice.

Online Communities:
Utilize online forums, social media groups, and websites dedicated to ADHD support. These platforms offer a space to ask questions, share experiences, and gain insights from a broader community.

Family and Friends:
Educate your immediate family and close friends about ADHD. Their understanding and support can make a significant difference. They can offer respite care, lend an empathetic ear, or help with day-to-day tasks.

School Collaboration:
Establish open communication with your child's school. Work with teachers, counselors, and special education professionals to create an Individualized Education Plan (IEP) or 504 Plan tailored to your child's needs.

Therapeutic Interventions:
Consider involving your child in therapy, such as behavioral therapy, to learn coping skills and

strategies for managing symptoms. These therapies can benefit not only your child but also you as a parent.

Parenting Workshops:
Attend workshops or classes specifically designed for parents of children with ADHD. These workshops can provide practical strategies for managing behavior, communication, and other challenges.

Counseling for Parents:
Remember that caring for a child with ADHD can be emotionally demanding. Seeking individual counseling or therapy for yourself can help you manage stress, frustration, and any feelings of isolation.

Self-Care:
Prioritize self-care to maintain your own physical and mental well-being. Engage in activities that recharge you and reduce stress. Taking care of yourself ensures you have the energy and patience to support your child.

Advocacy Groups:
Get involved with local or national advocacy groups focused on ADHD. These organizations can provide

resources, organize events, and help you raise awareness about ADHD-related issues.

Resilience and Flexibility:
Understand that challenges may arise, and not every strategy will work perfectly. Stay adaptable and resilient, and be willing to adjust your approach as your child's needs evolve.

Remember that building a support network takes time and effort. It's a process of trial and error as you find the resources and people who resonate with your situation. Ultimately, a strong support network can provide you with valuable guidance, validation, and a sense of community as you navigate the journey of parenting a child with ADHD.

Chapter 10

Advocating for your Child: Navigating the Education System and Legal Rights

Advocating for your child within the education system and understanding their legal rights is crucial for ensuring they receive the best possible education and support. Here's an in-depth guide to navigating this complex landscape:

1. Understanding the Education System:

Familiarize yourself with the structure of the education system in your region, including levels (elementary, middle, high school) and types (public, private, charter).
Research the curriculum, teaching methodologies, and extracurricular activities offered by schools to find the best fit for your child's needs.
2. Identifying Your Child's Needs:

Determine if your child has any special educational needs, disabilities, or learning differences that may require additional support.

Request assessments or evaluations to identify your child's strengths and challenges, which can guide the creation of an Individualized Education Plan (IEP) or a 504 Plan.

3. Individualized Education Plan (IEP) and 504 Plan:

An IEP is a legal document outlining specialized education goals and services for children with disabilities. Collaborate with school staff to create, review, and update the IEP regularly.

A 504 Plan provides accommodations and modifications for children with disabilities who do not require specialized instruction. Ensure the plan addresses your child's unique needs.

4. Researching Legal Rights:

Familiarize yourself with relevant laws, such as the Individuals with Disabilities Education Act (IDEA) and Section 504 of the Rehabilitation Act, to understand your child's rights to a free and appropriate education.

Research any state-specific laws or regulations that may apply to your situation.

5. Effective Communication:

Maintain open and respectful communication with teachers, counselors, and administrators. Regularly discuss your child's progress and any concerns you may have.

Keep written records of all interactions, including emails and meetings, for future reference.

6. Collaborating with Educators:

Collaborate with teachers to understand their teaching methods and classroom strategies. Share insights about your child's learning style and preferences.

Attend parent-teacher conferences and school events to establish a positive relationship with school staff.

7. Requesting Accommodations:

If your child requires accommodations, submit a formal request to the school in writing. Document the accommodations discussed and agreed upon.

Ensure the school is implementing the accommodations effectively and monitor their impact on your child's learning.

8. Resolving Disputes:

If disagreements arise, explore mediation or dispute resolution processes offered by the school or district.

If necessary, file a formal complaint with the appropriate education agency or consider seeking legal advice.

9. Seeking Additional Support:

Connect with local parent advocacy groups, disability organizations, or educational consultants who can provide guidance and support.

Attend workshops, seminars, and training sessions to stay informed about updates in education laws and practices.

10. Continual Monitoring and Adjustment:

Regularly review your child's progress and the effectiveness of their education plan. Make adjustments as needed to ensure their needs are being met.

Advocate for your child's evolving needs as they progress through different grade levels.

Remember, advocating for your child's education is an ongoing process that requires patience, persistence, and collaboration. By understanding their legal rights, effectively communicating with school personnel, and staying informed about best practices, you can help ensure your child receives the education they deserve.

10.1 Understanding Educational Rights and Accommodations for Children with ADHD

Children diagnosed with Attention Deficit Hyperactivity Disorder (ADHD) often face unique challenges in educational settings. Recognizing their rights and providing appropriate accommodations is essential for ensuring their academic success and overall well-being. This article delves into the comprehensive understanding of educational rights and accommodations for children with ADHD.

1. Definition and Impact of ADHD:
ADHD is a neurodevelopmental disorder characterized by symptoms of inattention, hyperactivity, and impulsivity. These symptoms can significantly impact a child's ability to focus, organize tasks, manage time, and regulate impulses. In an educational context, these challenges can affect learning, social interactions, and behavior.

2. Legal Framework:
In the United States, the Individuals with Disabilities Education Act (IDEA) and Section 504 of the Rehabilitation Act of 1973 provide the legal foundation for ensuring that students with disabilities, including

ADHD, receive appropriate educational services and accommodations. These laws mandate that schools offer a free and appropriate public education (FAPE) in the least restrictive environment.

3. Educational Rights:
Children with ADHD have the right to an Individualized Education Program (IEP) or a 504 Plan, depending on the severity of their condition. An IEP is a personalized document for students with disabilities that outlines specific educational goals, services, and accommodations. A 504 Plan provides accommodations and support to students with disabilities in a general education setting.

4. Eligibility for Services:
To be eligible for an IEP, the child's ADHD must adversely affect educational performance and require specialized instruction. A 504 Plan is typically considered when the child's condition substantially limits a major life activity, including learning. Evaluation by school professionals, medical experts, and parents' input is crucial in determining eligibility.

5. Accommodations and Support:
Accommodations for children with ADHD aim to level the playing field and address their specific challenges. Common accommodations include extended time on

assignments and tests, preferential seating, frequent breaks, use of assistive technology, and a structured daily routine. These accommodations help minimize the impact of ADHD-related difficulties.

6. Collaboration:
Effective collaboration between parents, teachers, school administrators, and support staff is crucial. This collaboration ensures that the child's needs are accurately identified and appropriately addressed. Regular communication and review of the child's progress help tailor accommodations as needed.

7. Advocacy:
Parents and guardians play a vital role in advocating for their child's educational rights. Understanding the child's needs, knowing their rights under the law, and communicating with school personnel are essential steps in ensuring the child's educational success.

8. Transition and Post-Secondary Education:
As children with ADHD approach high school graduation, transition planning becomes important. This planning includes preparing for post-secondary education, vocational training, or employment. It's crucial to continue advocating for appropriate accommodations and support during this transition.

9. Individualization:
Every child with ADHD is unique, and their needs may evolve over time. Therefore, it's essential to individualize accommodations and educational plans to address the child's specific strengths and challenges.

10. Inclusion and Empowerment:
The goal of providing educational rights and accommodations for children with ADHD is to empower them to reach their full potential. Inclusive education environments that recognize and address their needs contribute to their academic, social, and emotional growth.

In conclusion, understanding the educational rights and accommodations for children with ADHD is paramount to fostering an inclusive and supportive learning environment. By leveraging the legal framework, collaborating with stakeholders, and tailoring accommodations, we can ensure that children with ADHD have the opportunity to thrive academically and beyond.

10.2 Developing an Individualized Education Plan (IEP) or 504 Plan

Developing an Individualized Education Plan (IEP) or a 504 Plan involves a comprehensive process to ensure that students with disabilities receive appropriate support and accommodations in an educational setting. These plans are designed to address the unique needs of each student and enable them to access the curriculum and participate in school activities to the fullest extent possible.

1. Identifying the Need:
The process begins with identifying students who require additional support due to a disability. This could be a physical, intellectual, emotional, or developmental condition that affects their ability to learn and engage in a regular classroom environment.

2. Assessment:
A thorough assessment of the student's abilities, strengths, challenges, and specific needs is conducted. This may involve input from various professionals such as special education teachers, school psychologists, speech therapists, and medical

experts. The assessment helps determine the appropriate interventions and accommodations.

3. Setting Goals:
Based on the assessment, the IEP team, which includes parents, teachers, special education staff, and sometimes the student, sets specific and measurable goals that the student should achieve within a certain timeframe. These goals address academic, social, emotional, and behavioral areas.

4. Developing the Plan:
For an IEP, a detailed plan is created that outlines the student's current performance, identified needs, goals, services, and accommodations. It also specifies the role of each educator and the timeline for evaluating progress. For a 504 Plan, the focus is on accommodations that will ensure equal access to education, rather than specialized instruction.

5. Services and Accommodations:
IEPs often include specialized services such as speech therapy, occupational therapy, or one-on-one assistance. 504 Plans primarily list accommodations like extended time on tests, preferential seating, or access to assistive technology. These services and accommodations are tailored to the student's individual needs.

6. Implementation:
Teachers and other staff members responsible for the student's education are informed about the IEP or 504 Plan and their roles in its implementation. Regular communication among team members ensures that the plan is being carried out effectively.

7. Progress Monitoring and Review:
IEPs require periodic progress monitoring to determine whether the student is meeting their goals. Adjustments to the plan may be made based on the student's progress or changes in their needs. 504 Plans are reviewed less frequently, but adjustments can still be made as needed.

8. Transition Planning:
As students progress through their education, transition planning becomes crucial. For students with IEPs, transition plans are developed to ensure a smooth transition from high school to post-secondary education or employment.

In both cases, open communication between parents, educators, and the student (when appropriate) is essential to the success of the plan. The ultimate goal of both IEPs and 504 Plans is to provide students with the support they need to succeed academically and become active participants in their educational journey.

10.3 Communicating Effectively with School Personnel and Advocating for your Child's Needs

Communicating effectively with school personnel and advocating for your child's needs is a crucial aspect of ensuring your child receives the best possible education and support. Here's an in-depth guide on how to navigate this process:

Build Positive Relationships: Establishing positive relationships with teachers, counselors, and administrators is the foundation of effective communication. Attend parent-teacher conferences, school events, and open houses to connect with school staff and understand their perspectives.

Know Your Child's Needs: Clearly identify your child's strengths, weaknesses, learning styles, and any special needs they may have. This understanding will help you articulate your child's needs to school personnel.

Understand Education Laws: Familiarize yourself with relevant education laws such as the Individuals with Disabilities Education Act (IDEA) or Section 504 of the Rehabilitation Act. These laws protect the rights of students with disabilities and ensure they receive appropriate accommodations and services.

Gather Documentation: Collect relevant documentation such as assessment reports, medical records, and previous Individualized Education Plans (IEPs) or 504 Plans. These documents provide a clear picture of your child's needs and history.

Open Lines of Communication: Regularly communicate with teachers and school staff. Keep them informed about any changes in your child's circumstances that might affect their learning. Be approachable and open to suggestions.

Request Meetings: If you believe your child requires additional support, request meetings with teachers, counselors, and administrators. These meetings can address concerns and discuss possible solutions.

Prepare for Meetings: Before meetings, outline your concerns, questions, and desired outcomes. This will help you stay focused during the conversation and ensure that all relevant topics are covered.

Use Effective Communication Techniques: During meetings, communicate assertively but respectfully. Use "I" statements to express your concerns and avoid being confrontational. Focus on your child's needs and the desired outcomes.

Collaborate on Solutions: Work collaboratively with school personnel to brainstorm solutions that meet your child's needs. This could involve adjustments to the curriculum, extra support, or specialized services.

Request Accommodations: If your child has a documented disability, work with the school to create an Individualized Education Plan (IEP) or a 504 Plan. These plans outline specific accommodations and modifications to help your child succeed academically.

Follow Up: After meetings, follow up with school staff to track progress on the agreed-upon solutions. This shows your commitment to your child's education and helps ensure that changes are being implemented effectively.

Seek Professional Advice: If you encounter challenges, seek advice from professionals such as special education advocates or educational psychologists. They can provide insights and guidance on advocating for your child effectively.

Stay Informed: Keep yourself updated on your child's academic progress, attendance, and any behavioral issues. Regular communication with teachers will help you stay informed and proactive.

Maintain Records: Keep a record of all communications, meetings, and agreements with the school. This documentation can be valuable if conflicts arise or if you need to reference previous discussions.

Remember, effective communication and advocacy require patience, persistence, and a willingness to collaborate with school personnel. By actively participating in your child's education, you can help create a supportive learning environment that meets their unique needs.

10.4 Seeking Legal Support when Necessary

Seeking legal support is crucial when facing complex situations that require expert guidance and protection of your rights. Whether it's a personal matter, business issue, or any situation where legal implications are involved, obtaining professional legal advice is essential to navigate the complexities of the legal system.

Assessment of the Situation: Before seeking legal support, assess your situation to determine if legal intervention is necessary. If you're dealing with contracts, disputes, accidents, family matters, or criminal charges, consulting an attorney can help you understand your options and potential outcomes.

Choosing the Right Attorney: Once you've decided to seek legal assistance, it's vital to choose the right attorney for your specific needs. Look for an attorney with expertise in the relevant area of law. Research their experience, track record, and client reviews to ensure they are a good fit.

Initial Consultation: Many attorneys offer initial consultations to discuss your case and provide an overview of their services. Use this opportunity to ask questions about their approach, fees, and potential strategies. This will help you gauge their expertise and decide if you're comfortable working together.

Understanding Your Rights and Obligations: A lawyer will help you understand your rights and obligations in the context of your situation. They will provide insights into applicable laws and regulations, as well as potential legal strategies that could be employed.

Legal Strategy Development: Once you've engaged an attorney, they will work with you to develop a legal strategy tailored to your circumstances. They will outline the steps to be taken, the potential risks involved, and the possible outcomes.

Documentation and Paperwork: Legal matters often involve a significant amount of documentation and paperwork. Your attorney will assist in preparing and reviewing documents, contracts, and agreements to ensure they are accurate and protect your interests.

Negotiations and Settlements: If your case involves negotiations or potential settlements, your attorney will represent your best interests during discussions.

They will aim to achieve the most favorable outcome possible while considering your long-term goals.

Representation in Court: In cases that proceed to court, your attorney will represent you before a judge or jury. They will present your case, cross-examine witnesses, and argue on your behalf. Their experience and legal knowledge play a crucial role in presenting a strong case.

Legal Research: Attorneys conduct extensive legal research to gather precedents, statutes, and case law relevant to your situation. This research informs their arguments and strategies, strengthening your position.

Costs and Fees: Legal services come at a cost, and it's essential to discuss fees and payment arrangements with your attorney upfront. Some attorneys charge hourly rates, while others work on a contingency basis or offer fixed fees for specific services.

Confidentiality: Your attorney is bound by attorney-client privilege, meaning they are legally obligated to keep your communications confidential. This protection allows you to share sensitive information without fear of it being used against you.

Alternative Dispute Resolution: In some cases, attorneys may suggest alternative dispute resolution methods like mediation or arbitration to avoid lengthy court battles. These methods can be more cost-effective and faster than traditional litigation.

In conclusion, seeking legal support is a well-advised step when legal complexities arise. A qualified attorney can provide the expertise, guidance, and representation necessary to protect your rights and achieve the best possible outcome in various legal matters.

Chapter 11

Balancing Parenting and Self-care: Taking Care of Yourself as a Parent of an ADHD child

Balancing parenting and self-care while caring for a child with ADHD can be challenging, but it's crucial for both your well-being and your child's. Here's an in-depth look at strategies to effectively manage both responsibilities:

Education and Understanding:
Start by learning about ADHD to better understand your child's condition. This will help you manage their behaviors and needs more effectively.

Seek Professional Help:
Work closely with healthcare professionals, including pediatricians, therapists, and specialists. They can provide guidance, medication management, and behavioral interventions.

Consistent Routine:
Establish a structured daily routine for your child. Predictable schedules can help manage their symptoms and reduce stress for both you and your child.

Self-Care Prioritization:
Recognize that taking care of yourself isn't selfish; it's necessary. Prioritize self-care activities like exercise, hobbies, socializing, and relaxation.

Support Network:
Build a strong support network of friends, family, and other parents who understand your challenges. This network can provide emotional support and practical advice.

Effective Communication:
Openly communicate with your partner about responsibilities and needs. Sharing the load can prevent burnout and strengthen your partnership.

Set Realistic Expectations:
Understand that your child's behavior may be different due to ADHD. Set realistic expectations and celebrate small victories.

Delegate Tasks:
Don't hesitate to delegate tasks or ask for help. Share responsibilities with your partner, involve your child in age-appropriate chores, or hire assistance if needed.

Time Management:
Develop effective time management skills to balance your child's needs, your own responsibilities, and personal time. Tools like planners and apps can be useful.

Mindfulness and Stress Reduction:
Practice mindfulness, meditation, or yoga to manage stress. These techniques can help you stay present, reduce anxiety, and make better decisions.

Individual Time with Your Child:
Dedicate individualized time to your child regularly. This focused attention can help strengthen your bond and boost their self-esteem.

Celebrate Progress:
Celebrate your child's achievements and progress, no matter how small. Positive reinforcement encourages them and reduces frustration.

Flexibility and Adaptability:

Be prepared to adapt your strategies as your child's needs change. Flexibility is key to effectively managing the challenges of ADHD.

Patience and Self-Compassion:
Be patient with both yourself and your child. Remember that parenting is a journey, and it's okay to make mistakes.

Professional Support for Yourself:
Consider seeking counseling or therapy for yourself. A mental health professional can provide tools to manage stress and help you navigate the unique challenges you face.

Balancing parenting and self-care when raising a child with ADHD requires commitment, flexibility, and a strong support system. By prioritizing your well-being and effectively managing your child's needs, you can create a harmonious environment that benefits both you and your family.

11.1 Recognizing the Importance of Self-care for Parents

Self-care for parents is a crucial and often overlooked aspect of maintaining physical, emotional, and mental well-being. The demanding responsibilities of parenthood can leave little time for self-care, but recognizing its importance is essential for both parents and their children. Let's delve into the in-depth significance of self-care for parents:

Physical Health: Parenting can be physically taxing, with sleepless nights, constant running around, and the strain of lifting and carrying a child. Engaging in regular exercise, eating a balanced diet, and getting sufficient sleep are all fundamental components of self-care. By prioritizing their physical health, parents can sustain the energy levels needed to effectively care for their children.

Emotional Well-being: Parenting is emotionally demanding, often accompanied by feelings of joy, frustration, worry, and stress. Neglecting one's emotional needs can lead to burnout and negatively impact parent-child interactions. Taking time for hobbies, connecting with friends, or seeking professional help if needed can contribute to emotional balance, fostering a healthier parent-child relationship.

Mental Health: The constant juggling of responsibilities can take a toll on parents' mental health. Practicing mindfulness, meditation, or engaging in activities that promote relaxation can help alleviate stress and anxiety. A stable mental state allows parents to make informed decisions and respond thoughtfully to challenging situations.

Setting a Positive Example: Children learn by observing their parents' behavior. When parents prioritize self-care, they model the importance of maintaining personal well-being. This valuable lesson equips children with the tools to manage their own physical and emotional health as they grow.

Preventing Burnout: Continuous caregiving without breaks can lead to parental burnout. Burnout negatively impacts not only parents' well-being but also their ability to provide adequate care for their children. Regular self-care routines help prevent burnout by allowing parents to recharge and approach their responsibilities with renewed energy.

Enhancing Relationships: Healthy relationships with partners, family, and friends are vital for parents. Taking time for social connections, date nights, or quality time with loved ones contributes to overall happiness and provides a support network during challenging times.

Personal Fulfillment: While parenthood is fulfilling, it's essential for parents to nurture their individual interests and passions. Pursuing hobbies and activities they enjoy fosters a sense of personal fulfillment and identity beyond the role of a parent.

Coping Mechanisms: Life is full of unexpected challenges. When parents practice self-care, they develop effective coping mechanisms that enable them to navigate stressors and uncertainties more resiliently.

In conclusion, recognizing the importance of self-care for parents goes beyond simple relaxation; it is a foundational aspect of effective parenting. Prioritizing physical, emotional, and mental well-being not only benefits parents directly but also positively influences their ability to care for and nurture their children. It's essential for parents to view self-care not as a luxury, but as a necessity for their overall health and the well-being of their families.

11.2 Managing Stress and Overwhelm on parenting adhd child

Parenting a child with ADHD can indeed be challenging, but with the right strategies and support, it can also be incredibly rewarding. Here are some in-depth tips for managing stress and overwhelm while parenting a child with ADHD:

Education and Understanding: One of the first steps is to educate yourself about ADHD. Understand the symptoms, challenges, and treatment options. This knowledge will help you approach your child's behavior with empathy and patience.

Set Realistic Expectations: Recognize that your child's behavior may differ from that of neurotypical children. Set realistic expectations for their behavior, academic performance, and social interactions.

Structured Routine: Children with ADHD thrive on routines. Establish a structured daily routine that includes regular meal times, homework sessions, playtime, and bedtime. Consistency can help reduce stress for both you and your child.

Break Tasks into Smaller Steps: Break down tasks into smaller, manageable steps. This can prevent your child from feeling overwhelmed and make tasks more achievable.

Use Visual Aids: Visual schedules, charts, and reminders can help your child understand and follow routines. These visual aids can serve as gentle prompts for tasks they need to complete.

Positive Reinforcement: Use a system of positive reinforcement to encourage desired behavior. Offer rewards, praise, or privileges when your child follows routines, completes tasks, or demonstrates self-control.

Effective Communication: Maintain open and clear communication with your child. Use simple and direct language, and offer specific instructions. Avoid long lectures, as children with ADHD might struggle to focus.

Provide Breaks: Allow your child to take short breaks during activities that require focus. These breaks can help them recharge and maintain better attention.

Mindfulness and Relaxation: Teach your child relaxation techniques such as deep breathing, progressive muscle relaxation, or guided imagery. These techniques can help them manage stress and improve self-regulation.

Healthy Lifestyle: Ensure your child gets enough sleep, eats a balanced diet, and engages in regular physical activity. A healthy lifestyle can positively impact their ADHD symptoms.

Seek Professional Help: Consult with a pediatrician or mental health professional experienced in ADHD. They can provide guidance on medication if necessary and offer strategies for managing specific challenges.

Parental Self-Care: Don't forget about your own well-being. Parenting a child with ADHD can be exhausting, so prioritize self-care. Take breaks, engage in activities you enjoy, and seek support from friends, family, or support groups.

Problem-Solving Skills: Teach your child problem-solving skills. Help them identify challenges, brainstorm solutions, and evaluate the effectiveness of different strategies.

Advocate for Your Child: Work with your child's school to create an Individualized Education Plan (IEP) or a 504 Plan. These plans outline accommodations and support that can help your child succeed academically.

Celebrate Progress: Celebrate both small and significant achievements. Recognizing your child's efforts can boost their self-esteem and motivation.

Remember, every child with ADHD is unique, so it might take time to find what strategies work best for your child. Stay patient, adaptable, and willing to learn as you navigate the journey of parenting a child with ADHD.

11.3 Seeking Support and Resources for adhd Parents

Parenting a child with ADHD can be both rewarding and challenging. Seeking support and resources as a parent can make a significant difference in managing the unique needs of your child. Here's an in-depth guide to help you navigate this journey:

Education and Understanding:
Begin by learning about ADHD. Understand its symptoms, challenges, and how it affects your child's behavior, learning, and emotions. Knowledge empowers you to be an effective advocate for your child.

Professional Guidance:
Consult a qualified medical professional, such as a pediatrician, child psychiatrist, or psychologist, for an accurate diagnosis and tailored treatment plan. They can offer strategies, medications, and therapies to manage symptoms effectively.

Support Groups:
Join local or online support groups for parents of children with ADHD. Connecting with others who face similar challenges can provide a sense of community, empathy, and shared experiences.

Parenting Workshops:
Look for workshops, seminars, or webinars focused on parenting children with ADHD. These events often provide practical strategies, behavior management techniques, and communication skills to enhance your parenting approach.

Therapies:

Explore different therapies, such as behavior therapy, cognitive-behavioral therapy (CBT), or social skills training. These therapies can help your child develop coping skills, manage impulsivity, and improve self-esteem.

Educational Support:
Collaborate with your child's school to develop an Individualized Education Plan (IEP) or a 504 plan. These plans outline accommodations and modifications that can support your child's learning and success in the classroom.

Parenting Books:
There are numerous books written by experts and experienced parents that offer insights, strategies, and advice on parenting children with ADHD. Some popular titles include "The Explosive Child" by Ross W. Greene and "Smart but Scattered" by Peg Dawson and Richard Guare.

Online Resources:
Utilize reputable online platforms and websites dedicated to ADHD parenting. These resources often provide articles, videos, and downloadable materials covering a wide range of topics.

Behavior Management Techniques:

Learn about positive behavior reinforcement, time-outs, and structured routines. These techniques can help you manage impulsive behavior and encourage positive habits.

Self-Care:
Remember that taking care of yourself is essential. Parenting a child with ADHD can be demanding, so prioritize your physical, emotional, and mental well-being. Seek time for relaxation, hobbies, and spending quality time with your partner or other family members.

Advocacy:
Become an advocate for your child's needs in various settings, including school, extracurricular activities, and medical appointments. Communicate effectively with teachers, caregivers, and healthcare professionals to ensure your child's needs are met.

Parent-Teacher Collaboration:
Maintain open communication with your child's teachers. Regularly discuss your child's progress, challenges, and any adjustments that might be needed in the classroom.

Remember, every child with ADHD is unique, so tailor your approach to your child's specific needs and strengths. By seeking out resources, support, and education, you're taking proactive steps toward creating a positive and nurturing environment for your child to thrive.

11.4 Celebrating Your Child's Unique Abilities and Strengths

Celebrating your child's unique abilities and strengths is a crucial aspect of their emotional and psychological development. By acknowledging and nurturing their individual talents, you can help build their self-esteem, confidence, and overall well-being. Here's an in-depth exploration of this topic:

Recognition of Uniqueness:
Start by recognizing that every child is unique. Each child possesses a distinct set of abilities, interests, and strengths. It's essential to avoid comparing your child with others and instead focus on their personal growth journey.

Observation and Understanding:
Spend time observing your child's behavior, interests, and activities. This will help you identify their natural talents and strengths. Engage in conversations to

understand their passions and what activities bring them joy.

Creating a Supportive Environment:
Foster an environment that encourages exploration and development of your child's talents. Provide them with the necessary tools, resources, and opportunities to refine their skills and interests.

Positive Reinforcement:
Offer genuine praise and positive reinforcement when your child engages in activities that showcase their strengths. This boosts their self-confidence and motivates them to continue pursuing their passions.

Setting Realistic Expectations:
While it's important to encourage your child, ensure that you set realistic expectations. Pushing them too hard or placing excessive pressure on them could lead to burnout and a negative experience.

Balancing Challenges:
Encourage your child to step out of their comfort zone and take on challenges that align with their strengths. This helps them build resilience and learn that setbacks are a natural part of growth.

Open Communication:
Maintain open communication with your child about their interests and aspirations. Regularly check in with them to understand how they feel about their pursuits and if they need any additional support.

Providing Learning Opportunities:
Enroll your child in classes, workshops, or extracurricular activities related to their strengths. This exposure can help them develop their skills further and connect with peers who share similar interests.

Celebrating Progress:
Celebrate small victories along the way. Whether it's mastering a new skill, completing a project, or overcoming a challenge, these milestones deserve recognition and celebration.

Encouraging Perseverance:
Teach your child the value of perseverance and hard work. Let them know that success often comes from consistent effort and a willingness to learn from failures.

Embracing Diversity of Strengths:

Emphasize that strengths come in various forms. While some children may excel in academics, others might shine in sports, arts, or interpersonal skills. Encourage your child to appreciate the diversity of strengths in themselves and others.

Being a Role Model:
Lead by example. Share your own experiences of identifying and nurturing your strengths. This can help your child understand that the journey of self-discovery is ongoing.

Supporting Autonomy:
As your child grows, allow them to take ownership of their pursuits. Offer guidance when needed, but also give them the freedom to make decisions about their interests.

Lifelong Learning Mindset:
Instill a mindset of lifelong learning. Help your child understand that their strengths can evolve over time, and they should remain open to exploring new interests and passions.

In summary, celebrating your child's unique abilities and strengths involves creating an environment of support, recognition, and growth. By nurturing their passions and helping them build on their strengths, you can empower your child to develop into a confident, well-rounded individual.

Chapter 12

Looking Towards the Future: Preparing for Transitions and Independence

Preparing for the transitions and independence of your child with ADHD requires careful planning and consideration. Here are some key points to keep in mind:

Education and Advocacy:

Stay informed about your child's rights and accommodations available in the education system.
Foster self-advocacy skills so they can communicate their needs effectively.
Work with teachers to develop an Individualized Education Program (IEP) or 504 Plan that addresses their unique challenges.
Executive Functioning Skills:

Focus on developing executive functioning skills like time management, organization, planning, and prioritization.

Teach strategies such as using planners, setting reminders, and breaking tasks into smaller steps.

Emotional Regulation:

Help your child understand and manage their emotions through techniques like mindfulness, deep breathing, and positive self-talk.

Encourage open communication about their feelings and challenges.

Social Skills:

Offer opportunities for social interaction to improve social skills. This could include clubs, sports, or group activities.

Teach them how to read social cues and respond appropriately.

Transition Planning:

Plan ahead for major life transitions such as moving from high school to college or entering the workforce.

Visit colleges, explore career options, and consider internships or job shadowing to provide exposure.

Medication and Treatment:

Consult with medical professionals to determine the most suitable treatment plan, which may include medication, therapy, or a combination.
Ensure your child understands their treatment and is responsible for managing it.
Independent Living Skills:

Gradually teach skills needed for independent living, such as cooking, cleaning, budgeting, and basic home maintenance.
Self-Care and Wellness:

Emphasize the importance of a healthy lifestyle through regular exercise, balanced nutrition, and sufficient sleep.
Encourage hobbies and interests that promote well-being.
Career and Vocational Planning:

Identify strengths and interests to guide career choices.
Help them research potential careers and educational paths that align with their goals.
Financial Literacy:

Teach financial literacy skills such as budgeting, saving, and responsible spending.

Prepare them for managing their own finances as they become more independent.
Support Network:

Foster a supportive network of friends, mentors, and family members who understand their challenges and can provide guidance.
Goal Setting:

Assist your child in setting realistic short-term and long-term goals. Celebrate their achievements along the way.
Remember, every child is unique, and their journey toward independence will vary. Tailor your approach to your child's strengths, challenges, and preferences. Regular communication, patience, and a positive attitude will go a long way in helping them succeed in their transition to independence.

12.1 Transitioning from Childhood to Adolescence with ADHD

Transitioning from childhood to adolescence can be a complex process, and when ADHD is in the picture, it introduces additional considerations. ADHD, or Attention-Deficit/Hyperactivity Disorder, is a neurodevelopmental condition characterized by persistent patterns of inattention, impulsivity, and hyperactivity that can impact various aspects of an individual's life.

During the transition from childhood to adolescence, individuals with ADHD often experience a unique set of challenges. The cognitive and emotional changes that naturally occur during this period can interact with the symptoms of ADHD, potentially intensifying certain difficulties. Some key points to consider include:

Cognitive Changes: Adolescence is marked by increased demands on executive functions such as organization, planning, and time management. These areas are already challenging for individuals with ADHD due to impaired working memory and attention regulation. As academic responsibilities grow, adolescents with ADHD may struggle to cope with complex assignments and long-term projects.

Social and Emotional Dynamics: Peer relationships become more important during adolescence. Individuals with ADHD may face challenges in social interactions due to impulsive behavior or difficulty reading social cues. This can lead to feelings of rejection, low self-esteem, and heightened emotional sensitivity.

Impulse Control: Adolescents with ADHD might find it more difficult to manage impulsive behavior as they seek more independence. Risk-taking behaviors, such as experimenting with substances or engaging in unsafe activities, can be more pronounced in individuals with ADHD.

Academic Performance: Transitioning to middle or high school involves greater academic demands. Adolescents with ADHD may struggle with organization and time management, affecting their ability to complete assignments and study effectively. These challenges can lead to academic underachievement and increased stress.

Treatment Continuation: As individuals transition to adolescence, they may need to reassess their ADHD treatment plan. The effectiveness of previous interventions may change, and adolescents might need to explore new strategies for managing symptoms. Open communication between the individual, their caregivers, and healthcare providers is crucial in making informed decisions.

Coexisting Mental Health Conditions: Adolescence is a time when coexisting mental health conditions like anxiety and depression often emerge. These conditions can interact with ADHD symptoms, complicating the overall picture and requiring a comprehensive treatment approach.

Self-Advocacy and Autonomy: Adolescents with ADHD benefit from developing self-advocacy skills and taking ownership of their treatment. Educating them about their condition, teaching them coping strategies, and encouraging them to communicate their needs can empower them to navigate challenges more effectively.

In navigating the transition from childhood to adolescence with ADHD, a holistic approach is essential. This includes collaboration between parents, educators, mental health professionals, and the individual themselves. Tailoring support to address the specific needs and challenges of adolescents with ADHD can help them build resilience, develop effective coping strategies, and achieve success in various aspects of their lives.

12.2 Preparing your adhd child for High School and College

Preparing a child with ADHD for the transition to high school and college involves a multifaceted approach that considers their academic, social, and emotional needs. Here are some in-depth strategies to help ensure a successful transition:

Education and Advocacy:

Understand your child's ADHD diagnosis, strengths, and challenges. Share this information with teachers, counselors, and school staff to create an informed support network.
Work with the school's special education department to develop an Individualized Education Plan (IEP) or a 504 Plan. These documents outline accommodations and support tailored to your child's needs.
Executive Functioning Skills:

Help your child develop time management, organization, and planning skills. Use tools like planners, calendars, and digital apps to create routines and schedules.

Teach strategies for breaking tasks into manageable steps and prioritizing assignments. Encourage them to use checklists and reminders.

Study Strategies:

Teach effective study techniques such as active reading, note-taking, and summarizing. These strategies can enhance information retention and comprehension.

Encourage the use of visual aids, mind maps, and color-coding to organize information and enhance memory recall.

Self-Advocacy and Communication:

Empower your child to communicate their needs to teachers and professors. This could involve discussing accommodations, asking for clarification, or seeking additional help when needed.

Role-play different scenarios to help your child practice self-advocacy skills and build confidence in expressing their requirements.

Emotional Regulation:

Equip your child with techniques to manage stress and anxiety. This could include deep breathing exercises, mindfulness, or physical activities that promote relaxation.

Foster open communication about their emotions and encourage seeking help from counselors or therapists if needed.
Social Skills:

Help your child develop social skills through role-playing, practicing conversations, and joining extracurricular activities they're interested in.
Encourage positive relationships and peer interactions. Address any issues promptly and provide guidance on conflict resolution.
Healthy Lifestyle:

Emphasize the importance of a balanced diet, regular exercise, and adequate sleep. These factors can significantly impact attention, focus, and overall well-being.
Minimize excessive screen time, especially before bedtime, as it can disrupt sleep patterns.
Transition Planning:

Gradually introduce your child to the new environment. Visit the high school or college campus, meet teachers or professors, and familiarize them with the layout.
Discuss expectations and potential challenges related to the transition. Encourage them to share their concerns and brainstorm solutions together.

Continued Monitoring:

Maintain regular communication with teachers and counselors to monitor your child's progress. Adjust strategies and accommodations as necessary.
Stay involved in your child's education by reviewing assignments, grades, and providing ongoing guidance.
Celebrating Achievements:

Acknowledge your child's accomplishments and efforts, no matter how small. Celebrate milestones and successes to boost their self-esteem and motivation.
Remember that each child with ADHD is unique, and the strategies that work best may vary. Flexibility, patience, and ongoing support are key to helping your child navigate the challenges and excel in high school and college.

12.3 Nurturing Independence and Self-Advocacy Skills for your adhd child

Nurturing independence and self-advocacy skills in a child with ADHD requires a thoughtful and patient approach. Here's an in-depth guide to help you navigate this process:

Understanding ADHD: Begin by educating yourself about ADHD. Understand the specific challenges your child might face in terms of impulsivity, hyperactivity, and attention difficulties. This knowledge will help you tailor your approach to their needs.

Set Realistic Expectations: Recognize that building independence and self-advocacy skills might take longer for children with ADHD. Set achievable goals and be prepared for progress to be gradual.

Structured Environment: Create a structured and predictable environment at home. Consistent routines and schedules can help children with ADHD better manage their time and activities.

Teach Organizational Skills: Break tasks into smaller, manageable steps. Teach your child to use tools like checklists, planners, and calendars to keep track of their tasks and responsibilities.

Skill-Building Activities: Engage in activities that promote executive functioning skills, such as planning, organizing, and decision-making. Cooking, arts and crafts, and interactive games can all be used to foster these skills.

Practice Time Management: Help your child understand the concept of time through timers, alarms, or visual cues. Gradually encourage them to manage their time on their own for tasks like homework or chores.

Self-Monitoring: Teach your child to monitor their own behaviors and reactions. Encourage self-reflection and discuss their experiences, both positive and challenging.

Problem-Solving Skills: Guide your child through problem-solving techniques. When they encounter difficulties, help them brainstorm potential solutions and evaluate the outcomes.

Effective Communication: Teach assertiveness and effective communication skills. Encourage your child to express their needs and concerns openly, while also practicing active listening.

Self-Advocacy Skills: Equip your child with knowledge about their ADHD diagnosis. Help them understand their strengths and challenges, and empower them to communicate their needs to teachers, peers, and other adults.

Role Modeling: Model the behaviors you want your child to adopt. Demonstrate self-advocacy, organization, and decision-making skills in your own life.

Celebrate Progress: Acknowledge and celebrate even small steps towards independence and self-advocacy. Positive reinforcement can motivate your child to continue developing these skills.

Professional Guidance: Consider involving a therapist or counselor with experience in ADHD. They can provide tailored strategies and support to both you and your child.

Flexibility and Patience: Be patient with setbacks. Building independence is a gradual process, and your child might face hurdles along the way. Approach challenges with flexibility and a positive attitude.

Encourage Interests: Support your child's interests and hobbies. Engaging in activities they're passionate about can boost their self-esteem and provide opportunities for skill development.

Remember, every child is unique, and what works best may vary. Regularly assess and adjust your approach based on your child's progress and needs.

With time, consistent effort, and your unwavering support, your child can develop the independence and self-advocacy skills they need to thrive.

12.4 Embracing a Positive Outlook on the Future for Children with ADHD

Embracing a positive outlook for children with ADHD is essential for their well-being and development. ADHD, or Attention Deficit Hyperactivity Disorder, is a neurodevelopmental condition that affects a child's ability to focus, control impulses, and manage hyperactivity. While it presents challenges, fostering a positive perspective can make a significant difference in their lives.

Understanding ADHD: Educating parents, teachers, and caregivers about the nature of ADHD is crucial. Recognizing that it's not just a matter of willpower but a neurobiological condition helps shift the focus from blame to support.

Early Intervention: Identifying ADHD early allows for timely intervention. Early diagnosis leads to tailored strategies that help children manage their symptoms effectively and build essential skills.

Strengths-Based Approach: Recognizing and nurturing the strengths of children with ADHD is paramount. They often possess traits like creativity, spontaneity, and a unique way of thinking that can lead to success in various fields.

Personalized Learning: Embracing individualized education plans can help children learn in ways that suit their learning style and pace, enabling them to thrive academically and socially.

Building Self-Esteem: Focusing on achievements, no matter how small, can boost a child's self-esteem. Encouraging a growth mindset, where effort is celebrated, helps them develop resilience and a positive self-image.

Effective Communication: Open communication between parents, teachers, and therapists fosters a supportive environment. Sharing insights and working collaboratively ensures consistent strategies for managing ADHD symptoms.

Mindfulness and Coping Strategies: Teaching mindfulness techniques and coping strategies empowers children to manage impulsivity, improve focus, and handle emotional challenges.

Physical Activity: Regular exercise can help reduce hyperactivity and improve concentration. Encouraging participation in sports or physical activities supports their overall well-being.

Structured Routine: Establishing a consistent daily routine provides predictability and helps children manage their time and responsibilities more effectively.

Social Skills Development: Addressing social challenges through targeted interventions allows children to navigate social situations with more confidence, improving their relationships and reducing feelings of isolation.

Positive Role Models: Sharing stories of successful individuals with ADHD, such as entrepreneurs, artists, and athletes, offers inspiration and demonstrates that ADHD does not define one's potential.

Family Support: Providing parents and caregivers with resources, support groups, and training equips them with the tools to create a nurturing environment for their child's growth.

Medication and Therapy: For some children with ADHD, medication and therapy may be recommended. A positive outlook involves understanding that these interventions are tools that can support the child's development.

Celebrating Progress: Celebrating milestones and progress, regardless of the pace, reinforces the idea that improvement is a continuous journey.

Embracing a positive outlook for children with ADHD involves acknowledging their challenges while emphasizing their strengths and potential. By fostering understanding, providing tailored support, and cultivating an environment of patience and encouragement, we can help these children lead fulfilling lives and contribute their unique talents to society.